HORRIBLE SCIENCE

DANGER

MICROSCOPIC MONSTERS

Nick Arnold Illustrated by **Tony De Saulles**

■SCHOLASTIC

www.horrible-science.co.uk

Scholastic Children's Books,
Euston House, 24 Eversholt Street,
London NW1 1DB, UK

A division of Scholastic Ltd
London ~ New York ~ Toronto ~ Sydney ~ Auckland
Mexico City ~ New Delhi ~ Hong Kong

First published in the UK by Scholastic Ltd, 1996
Abridged edition first published by Scholastic Ltd, 2014
This edition published 2018

Text © Nick Arnold, 2001, 2004, 2018
Illustrations © Tony De Saulles, 2001, 2004
Index by Caroline Hamilton

ISBN 978 1407 18538 5

Printed and bound by CPI Group (UK) Ltd, Croydon, CR0 4YY

2 4 6 8 10 9 7 5 3 1

The right of Nick Arnold and Tony De Saulles to be identified as the author
and illustrator of this work respectively has been asserted by them in accordance
with the Copyright, Designs and Patents Act, 1988.

CONTENTS

Nick Arnold has been writing stories and books since he was a youngster, but never dreamt he'd find fame thanks to microscopic monsters. His research involved interviewing fleas and getting friendly with bacteria and he enjoyed every minute of it.

When he's not delving into Horrible Science, he spends his spare time eating pizza, riding his bike and thinking up corny jokes (though not all at the same time).

www.nickarnold-website.com

Tony De Saulles picked up his crayons when he was still in nappies and has been doodling ever since. He takes Horrible Science very seriously, even when he draws magnified toilet germs. Fortunately, he's made a full recovery. When he's not out with his sketchpad, Tony likes to write poetry and play squash, though he hasn't written any poetry about squash yet.

www.tonydesaulles.co.uk

INTRODUCTION

Which of these is the smallest?

a) Your pocket money.

MISERLY AMOUNT

b) Your teacher's brain.

PATHETICALLY PUNY

c) A mite (a bug that looks like a scaled-down spider).

TINY BUT TERRIFYING

Well, hopefully you said **c)** because at just 0.2 mm, a mite is one of the smallest objects anyone can see. Your eyes can't see smaller things because the lenses in your eyeballs can't focus on them. And that means that whatever you look at has a whole lot of detail that's too small to make out. This tiny world can be very incredible, and very beautiful (they say small is beautiful don't they?).

But it can also be very *horrible*!

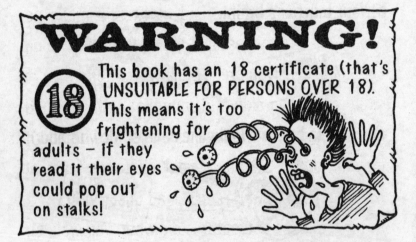

WARNING!

This book has an 18 certificate (that's UNSUITABLE FOR PERSONS OVER 18). This means it's too frightening for adults – if they read it their eyes could pop out on stalks!

Now, as I said, your eyes can't see tiny things, but your mind's eye can *imagine* them. And when you read this book your imagination will be working so hard there'll be steam coming out your ears! You'll be imagining a whole new world – the terribly tiny microscopic world. And as you're about to find out, it's a world of violence and sudden death.

Yes, it's a world of microscopic horrors and MONSTERS that make made-up monsters in stories appear loveable and fluffy. And make no mistake – the microscopic monsters in this book are as REAL as you are! At this very second they're strolling on your skin and snuggling into your bed and scoffing your sandwiches and splashing about in your toilet! So brace yourself for a feast of fearsomely fascinating facts. Find out…

- how millions of creatures *die* when you walk on the grass.

- what slimy animals lurk between your *teeth*.

- how germs can make dead bodies *explode*.

- and WORST OF ALL, how flushing the toilet can cover you in *poo*.

ANOTHER WARNING!
These facts could turn a frog green! And don't leave this book on Granny's chair – It could make her false teeth fall out!

No, you'd best read this book right now before someone else takes it away and starts reading it for themselves!

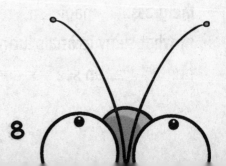

8

MAGICAL MICROSCOPES

To explore the weird world of microscopic monsters you'll need a magical machine.

THE MAGIC MICROSCOPE

If I said microscopes were magical you wouldn't believe me.

YEAH, RIGHT!

Quite right – magic isn't real! But when you peer through a microscope and see things that no human eye can see – it does *feel* like magic...

And just to prove it — here's an instant experiment. Try putting your eye close to this circle. Look closely...

○

Concentrate hard ... *very hard* ... do you see anything?

Well, that proves the limits of your human eyesight. Now turn to the next page for a microscope view of this tiny circle enlarged one hundred times... All this was under your nose and you never saw it!

So you know that paper is made up of little fibres that were once wood from trees? Well, here's your chance to check out what else you know…

A TINY, TINY QUIZ

This quiz is so easy that you're even told what the answers are! Trouble is, the letters in the answers are muddled up so you've got to work out what they say!

1 Whenever you ride your bike the tyres leave tiny microscopic traces of melted ... REBRUB.

2 A fungus makes microscopic seeds called spores. When the sun shines they go dark just like you do when you get a ... STUNNA.

3 When you go outside, your hair, your clothes and the snot in your nose become coated in thousands of microscopic bits of rock half the width of a hair. They're known as ... TRIG.

4 At the heart of every raindrop is a microscopic speck of dust. Some of this dust fell to Earth from ... ROUTE CAPES.

5 Look at a spider's web under a microscope and you'll see tiny lumps of ... GUEL.

6 All the tiny bits of dirt and dead skin that you've washed off your hair in your life would weigh more than your … HOWLE ODBY.

7 In 1848 scientist John Quekett peered through his microscope at a scrap of leather that had been nailed to a church door. He was shocked to discover it was really … UNHAM INKS.

UNHAM INKS! THAT'S DISGUSTING!

ANSWERS:

1 No, not rhubarb — it's RUBBER. When your tyres touch the road a tiny surface layer 0.025 mm (0.001 inches) thick melts — so in fact your wheel slides over the ground! The tyre cools immediately as the wheel turns away from the road but microscopic traces of rubber remain stuck to the tarmac. When your tyre

has lost lots of rubber it looks worn and tyred, I mean tired.

2 Are you stunned? It's a SUNTAN. Yes, fungal spores get suntans and the chemical that makes this dark colour is melanin — the same substance that makes the dark colour in human skin!

3 Yes, it's a TRIGY question. It's GRIT, made up of finely ground up rock or sand just 0.03 mm in size that's blown on the wind. Some grit comes from deserts or erupting volcanoes on the other side of the world! If it gets in your pudding you could have a bit of desert in your dessert!

4 Every day, millions of specks of dust about 0.002 mm across fall to Earth from OUTER SPACE. Inside a cloud drops of rain form around the dust and when a raindrop plops down the back of your neck you could be making contact with a 4.7 billion-year-old lump of alien rock! It's even older than your dad's favourite music — that's just ancient rock.

5 Do they serve GUEL in your school dinners? Actually, it's GLUE to stick insects to the web. Did you know that spider's silk is one of the strongest materials in the world — yet a spider's web that stretched around the world would weigh no more than an orange?

6 Don't 'HOWL ODDLY' — it's WHOLE BODY! In just one year you could collect 3 kg of grotty, greasy gunk from your hair. You could fill a small bucket and butter your sandwiches with it!

7 What do you INK this stuff is? It turned out to be HUMAN SKIN cut from a dead Viking 900 years before. Well, I'm sure the Viking was really cut up about that.

So how did you get on? If you thought it was easy then maybe you fancy really getting to grips with the microscopic world.

TEST YOUR TEACHER...

ANSWER

The correct answer is, "I dunno!" because no one is sure – but teachers don't like admitting they don't know things and historians don't mind guessing...

The truth is, ALL three *said* they invented the microscope. Well, I suppose anyone could have made the discovery. Once you've got a couple of lenses (the glass bits that make objects appear larger) it's easy enough to put them together and realize that two lenses make things appear larger than just one lens. And when your arms start aching from holding the lenses apart at the right distance to see tiny things in focus, sooner or later you'll hit on the idea of sticking the lenses at either end of a tube. And hey presto – you've invented the microscope!

But what about the lens? Well, guess what – no one's too sure who invented the lens either! We've brought some experts together to try and solve the mystery.

1 Archaeologists have found a piece of rock crystal in a cave on the island of Crete. It was carved 4,500 years ago.

IT'S SHAPED LIKE A LENS AND IT MAKES THINGS LOOK BIGGER!

2 In 1850 archaeologists found another lens-shaped crystal in what is now Iraq. It was carved by the Assyrian people in 800 BC.

MINE'S BETTER QUALITY - IT'S CRYSTAL CLEAR!

YES, BUT MINE'S OLDER!

3 Boring historians point out that there is no actual *proof* that these crystals were used as lenses at all.

But there is proof in the writings of short-sighted Roman philosopher Seneca (4 BC–AD 65) that he used a bowl of water as a lens to help him read the scrolls at his local library. So does that mean Seneca invented the lens?

IT'S TRANSPARENTLY OBVIOUS!

SOUNDS FISHY TO US!

LOVELY LENSES

Anyway, *someone* invented the lens and around 1300 someone else in Italy (yes, you guessed it, no one knows who) found out how to grind glass to make lenses. The trick was getting the right shape – wanna know how it's done? Well, why not make your own? Go on, it's easy!

DARE YOU DISCOVER ... HOW TO MAKE YOUR OWN LENS?

In the olden days you had to cut the glass carefully to shape and then grind it with gritty substances by hand until you had made exactly the right curve. And then you had to 'polish' it to get rid of any scratches. (Basically, this meant grinding the glass some more with fine powders.) This grinding might take days of toil.

But you'll be pleased to know there's an easier way...

You will need:

• A bottle shaped like this...
(An empty mouthwash bottle is ideal)

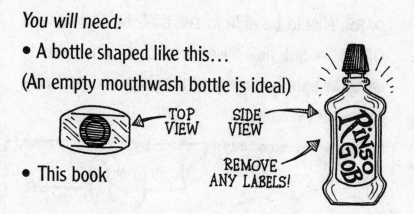

TOP VIEW

SIDE VIEW

• This book

REMOVE ANY LABELS!

What you do:

1 Completely fill the bottle with water so there are no air bubbles.

2 Place the bottle sideways on over this page, put your eye close to the bottle and look at this fascinating blood-sucking flea.

HURRY UP,
I HAVEN'T
GOT ALL DAY!

You should be able to see that the flea has got bigger – but how? Here's a clue: you have to imagine light bouncing off the page and bouncing into your eyeballs.

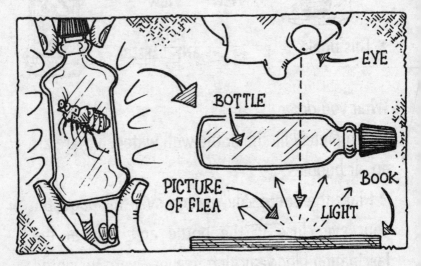

Which of these explanations is correct:
a) The light speeds up as it passes through water and this makes your brain think the flea is bigger than it is.

b) The water bends the light towards a point. If I put my eye at this point I can see the flea close up.
c) The water makes the light brighter and this makes my brain think that the flea is bigger.

ANSWER

b) Light bends as it passes through the bottle and the water and the angle the light hits your eye at fools your brain into thinking that the object is much nearer and so much larger than it really is. And that – surprise, surprise – is how a microscope lens works, only the bending of light is done by the glass.

For about 70 years after they were invented, microscopes weren't terribly powerful and few scientists had cottoned on to the potential of the new invention. But a lone genius was about to change all that. With his own hands he would make the most powerful microscopes then known and use them to make some monster discoveries...

Hall of fame: Antonie van Leeuwenhoek (1632–1723)

Nationality: Dutch

Leeuwenhoek means 'Lion's Corner' – which was the name of the café Antonie's dad owned in Delft, Holland. Oh well, things could have been worse. Antonie

EGG AND CHIPS READY FOR TABLE NINE!

could have been named after something on the menu – he might have had to go through life as 'Antonie Supa-dupa-whopper-burger'!

Antonie's dad died when he was still at school. The young boy went to live with a relative and learned how to be a cloth merchant. For much of his life he was a quietly hard-working, quietly prosperous shopkeeper in his home town of Delft. It sounds seriously boring but at least he had an interesting hobby…

You've guessed it! Microscopes!

Like other cloth sellers of the time, Antonie used a lens to check the quality of his wares. But unlike the others, Antonie was *seriously* into lenses. He learnt how to make lenses from tiny beads of glass and he mounted them on metal plates to make simple microscopes. Here's one now…

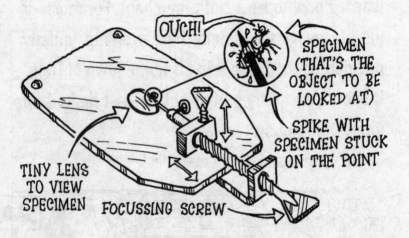

OUCH!

SPECIMEN (THAT'S THE OBJECT TO BE LOOKED AT)

SPIKE WITH SPECIMEN STUCK ON THE POINT

TINY LENS TO VIEW SPECIMEN

FOCUSSING SCREW

Antonie was very good at his work because he had incredibly sharp eyesight which was ideal for spotting tiny details and he was a very curious man – I mean curious in the sense of wanting to find out more about the tiny world. So he decided to use his microscope to look at other tiny things.

Before Leeuwenhoek, people had no idea that

things could happen on a scale too small for them to see. So they made up fanciful explanations for why things happen…

WHERE DO FLEAS COME FROM?

THEY FORM FROM DIRT!

I'VE BEEN ITCHING TO KNOW THAT!

But Leeuwenhoek saw flea eggs through his microscope and realized that's where fleas came from. (So it sounds like his work was up to scratch!) Then he looked at tiny baby eels and proved that people were wrong when they said that eels formed from dew. Yes, once again he 'dew' the right conclusion! Leeuwenhoek was so keen on his microscopes that he nearly blinded himself watching gunpowder explode at close quarters. And that nearly blew his chances of seeing anything!

As Antonie's excitement grew he wrote letters to the Royal Society, the top scientific club in Britain, and told them about his discoveries. Here's what one letter might have said (the letter was in Dutch but we've translated it)…

To Henry Oldenberg,
Secretary of
the Royal Society

September 1676

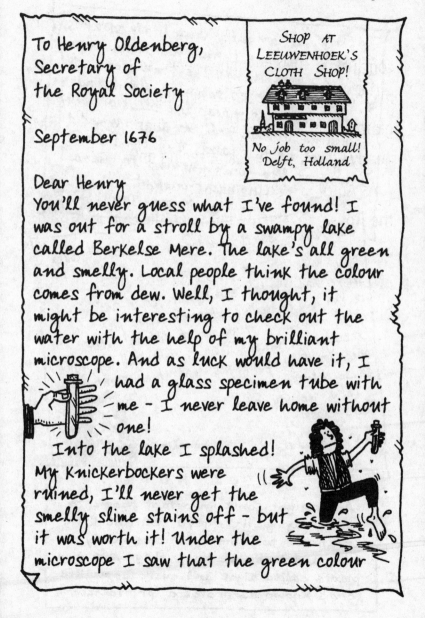

SHOP AT
LEEUWENHOEK'S
CLOTH SHOP!

No job too small!
Delft, Holland

Dear Henry

You'll never guess what I've found! I was out for a stroll by a swampy lake called Berkelse Mere. The lake's all green and smelly. Local people think the colour comes from dew. Well, I thought, it might be interesting to check out the water with the help of my brilliant microscope. And as luck would have it, I had a glass specimen tube with me – I never leave home without one!

Into the lake I splashed! My knickerbockers were ruined, I'll never get the smelly slime stains off – but it was worth it! Under the microscope I saw that the green colour

29

was actually tiny little strands, thinner than a hair. And there were things like tiny green raspberries swimming about and little creatures shaped like blobs of jelly squishing around. Well, my legs turned to jelly too. At this point, I realized I was looking at life forms unknown to science! Is this great or what? →

Yours, Tony

The Royal Society, London.   October 1676

Dear Antonie

We've had a chat about your letter and we reckon you're telling whopping porkie-pies. In other words, we think you're fibbing! Little creatures in water? Yeah – right, pull the other one! You'll be telling us that these creatures cause disease next!

Let's see you prove it – OK!?

Yours crossly,

Henry Oldenberg →

A QUICK NOTE...

Antonie got some important people to write saying that they'd seen the little creatures, too. The creatures really did exist and today we know they were tiny plants called algae and microscopic life forms known as protozoa (pro-toe-zo-a).

30

One day in 1683 Antonie made a bigger – or should I say smaller – breakthrough. He peered at gunk from between his teeth and saw tiny creatures. He was so excited he grabbed his wife and daughter and scraped their teeth-gunk too. So what would you do if your mad dad started messing with your teeth? Leeuwenhoek was over the moon – his family had creatures in their teeth! Surely that was enough? Not if you're a great scientist!

Leeuwenhoek grabbed two manky old men – they hadn't been near a toothbrush in their whole lives. Their teeth were brown and rotten and their breath could scare a skunk. The scientist held his nose and scraped grot from their gruesome gobs. The old mens' mouths were alive with horrible creatures all splashing about like fish in water. Leeuwenhoek was the first human to glimpse the things we call bacteria (for the slimy details see microbes page 100, bacteria page 102). But he wanted more – so he peered at his own poo and was thrilled to find more bacteria!

Leeuwenhoek wrote a book about his work and became famous. Soon kings and lords were rushing to his little shop and begging to look at germs. So could YOU follow in Leeuwenhoek's footsteps and become a great microscope scientist? To help you here's … the world's smallest ruler…

1 CM

YES, THIS IS IT!
USE IT TO
MEASURE SOME
TINCY WINCY
THINGS…

We've enlarged a bit so you can see it…

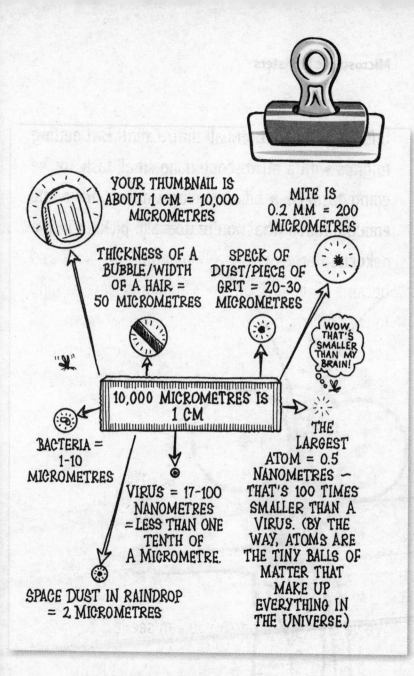

YOUR THUMBNAIL IS ABOUT 1 CM = 10,000 MICROMETRES

MITE IS 0.2 MM = 200 MICROMETRES

THICKNESS OF A BUBBLE/WIDTH OF A HAIR = 50 MICROMETRES

SPECK OF DUST/PIECE OF GRIT = 20-30 MICROMETRES

WOW, THAT'S SMALLER THAN MY BRAIN!

10,000 MICROMETRES IS 1 CM

BACTERIA = 1-10 MICROMETRES

VIRUS = 17-100 NANOMETRES = LESS THAN ONE TENTH OF A MICROMETRE.

THE LARGEST ATOM = 0.5 NANOMETRES — THAT'S 100 TIMES SMALLER THAN A VIRUS. (BY THE WAY, ATOMS ARE THE TINY BALLS OF MATTER THAT MAKE UP EVERYTHING IN THE UNIVERSE)

SPACE DUST IN RAINDROP = 2 MICROMETRES

33

Got your head round all that? Great! But getting to grips with a microscope is no small task. You're going to need a bit more know-how and, oddly enough, that's what you're going to pick up in the next chapter...

CRUCIAL MICROSCOPIC KNOW-HOW

In this chapter you can practise using a microscope and even follow in Leeuwenhoek's footsteps and make your own. But first, a quick jog down memory lane to the bad old days of microscopes. The days when your science teacher strutted around in a powdered wig and an embarrassing floppy cravat.

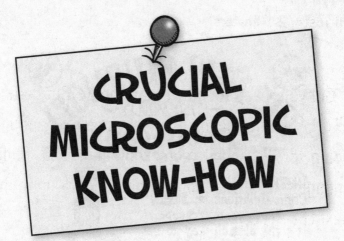

THE NEW BLURMORE
~ (1730 MODEL) ~
MICROSCOPE

INSTRUCTIONS

Congratulations on buying the Blurmore microscope. It's the hi-tech way to see very small things that we scientists don't really understand yet! Here's how to examine a slug...

1 Kill the slug and dry its body. Then soak it in blood. The blood will dry and harden around the slug. This way it's easy to cut its body into thin slices with a sharp knife to study its slimy innards.

2 Lay a slice of slug on a microscope slide. Add a few blobs of smelly glue made of boiled up fish-bones to hold your slug in position. If you happen to be out of fish you could try a blob of fat from a dead animal.

3 Now you are ready to look at your slide, so simply place it under the lens of your microscope and peer through the eyepiece!

GAZOOKS!

RE SMALL PRINT ~
1. Our lenses are rather blurry and colours appear in the glass like a rainbow and that makes it a bit confusing. But hey — it's pretty!
2. Your slide will quickly rot and become smelly.

THINGS COULD ONLY GET BETTER...

1 In 1830 microscope enthusiast Joseph Jackson Lister (1786–1869) designed a new type of microscope. It had two lenses fitted together and each lens was made out of a different type of glass. For complex reasons to do with the way light bends through the different types of glass, this cut out the confusing colours.

2 Also in the 1830s you could buy pure glass lenses that were clearer than the old types of glass which had traces of other chemicals that made them blurry. You could say the new lenses were clearly better!

3 Remember how you had to cut the specimen into thin slices? By the 1860s scientists had learnt how to cover the specimen in paraffin wax to hold it steady before they cut it. The idea made slicing easier and safer so I guess it proved a cut above the rest.

4 By the 1890s scientists were using a chemical called formalin to harden the specimen before the wax stage. The formalin preserved the specimen and made it easier to cut. The discovery was made by a scientist who was using formalin to kill germs on a dead mouse. But he absent-mindedly left the mouse in the formalin overnight and in the morning it was harder than a school cheese.

Today undertakers use formalin to preserve dead bodies but school cheeses are preserved using slightly less poisonous chemicals.

STILL WANT TO BE A MICROSCOPE EXPERT?

Wow, that's great! This magazine should be right up your eyepiece…

(PUBLISHED WEEKLY BY TERRIBLY ENTHUSIASTIC INC.)

MICRO-MAG

GETTING THE BEST FROM YOUR MICROSCOPE
by Howie Doitt

Hi, fellow microscope dudes! The microscope is a wonderfully wicked, cool invention! Here's a few dos and don'ts to get the very best from your machine!

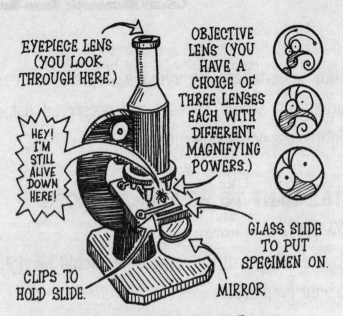

EYEPIECE LENS (YOU LOOK THROUGH HERE.)

OBJECTIVE LENS (YOU HAVE A CHOICE OF THREE LENSES EACH WITH DIFFERENT MAGNIFYING POWERS.)

HEY! I'M STILL ALIVE DOWN HERE!

GLASS SLIDE TO PUT SPECIMEN ON.

CLIPS TO HOLD SLIDE.

MIRROR

DOS AND DON'TS

DO

Shine a bright light on your microscope. The mirror will reflect light under the specimen. Of course, if the object is solid like the head of a dead insect you could try lighting the object from above otherwise it'll appear as a dark blob and you blobably won't see much.

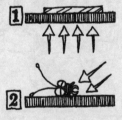

DO

Use a very soft cloth or air brush to remove dust from your microscope lenses. (Oh, by the way, an air brush is an air bulb with a brush attached. You

ERK!

squeeze the bulb and puff air to blow away that nasty dust and the brush gets rid of any sticky bits.) TLC for lenses — that's what I say!

DON'T

Lower your objective whilst looking through the eyepiece. The mere thought of this is enough to make me cry! You might get muck over your precious lens and you could even break through your glass specimen slide — BOO HOO!

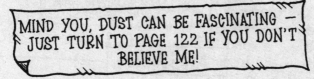

DON'T

Forget to replace the dust cap on your eyepiece and cover your microscope when it's not in use. Once again, dust might get on the lenses. And then all your observations could bite the dust...

MIND YOU, DUST CAN BE FASCINATING — JUST TURN TO PAGE 122 IF YOU DON'T BELIEVE ME!

MICROSCOPIC EXPRESSIONS

Two microscope scientists are talking…

> WAS THE DEPTH OF FIELD OK FOR THE BODY TUBE?

> YES – BUT I LACKED THE RESOLUTION!

Do you say…?

> HELP! THEY'VE MURDERED SOMEONE AND PUT THE BODY IN A TUBE AND THEN BURIED IT IN A FIELD AND ONE OF THEM IS FEELING SCARED!

ANSWER

Poppycock, codswallop, humbug! The body tube is the main part of a microscope that contains the lenses. Depth of field means the amount that you can move the body tube up and down and still get a clear image and resolution means the amount of detail you can see. D'you see?

BET YOU NEVER KNEW!

How scientists make slides of specimens...

1 They stain the specimen so it shows up really clearly under the microscope. A stain is a special dye that colours certain chemicals and shows up certain parts of the tiny object the scientist is looking at. A commonly used stain is cochineal – made from ground beetles!

GULP!

NEXT!

2 Cut a thin slice of the object. That's so that the light can shine through it from below and you can see it clearly under the microscope. How thin? Well about one thousandth of a millimetre (one micrometre) will do. Scientists use a tool called a microtome to do the cutting – and I expect very mean scientists use it to cut cake.

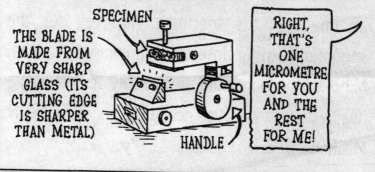

SPECIMEN

THE BLADE IS MADE FROM VERY SHARP GLASS (ITS CUTTING EDGE IS SHARPER THAN METAL)

HANDLE

RIGHT, THAT'S ONE MICROMETRE FOR YOU AND THE REST FOR ME!

3 They place the specimen on a glass with a drop of water to stop it drying out and a thin piece of glass called a cover slip to protect it. Or if they want to store the specimen they might cover it in glycerine and gelatine and seal the edges of the cover slip with gum arabic to stop it from drying or rotting.

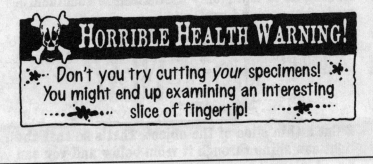

HORRIBLE HEALTH WARNING!

Don't you try cutting *your* specimens! You might end up examining an interesting slice of fingertip!

Nowadays, many microscopes are digital. A light sensor a bit like the one in a digital camera forms an image of the specimen. And you see the specimen horribly close-up on a computer screen. Mind you, if you want to see tiny terrors like a deadly disease virus you need to use an ELECTRON MICROSCOPE.

Here's how to make your own...

Microscopic monsters fact file

Name:

Basic facts:

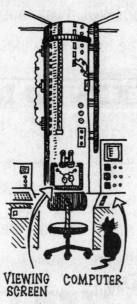

VIEWING COMPUTER
SCREEN

Monstrous details:

BEE'S KNEES

DEADLY VIRUS

Electron microscope

1 An electron microscope fires electrons at the object you're looking at. (Electrons are the tiny blips of energy that surround atoms.)

2 Like electrons, light is made of tiny blips of energy but they zig-zag very fast to form light waves. If the object is smaller than a light wave (0.5 micrometres) then your eyes won't be able to see it with an ordinary microscope.

3 The beam of electrons is far smaller than a light wave. So you can actually study objects 200,000 times smaller than with an ordinary microscope.

An electron microscope is fab for looking at really horrible tiny objects. Things like the viruses that cause deadly diseases such as rabies.

HOW TO BUILD YOUR OWN SCANNING ELECTRON MICROSCOPE

Wanna get closer to the action? Well, if your answer is, "Not 'arf" then you've come to the right place!

WARNING!

Please read these directions before you get started. But beware: some of them might not be very sensible!

First assemble your materials…

A large metal pipe. (A sewer pipe will do – better give it a good scrub!)

A fluorescent screen and electron gun from an old-fashioned box-shaped TV set. You might find one covered in dust in your school storeroom…

Some *very* powerful magnets.

A computer. (It needs software suitable for presenting pictures from an electron microscope. Perhaps a friendly computer programmer could knock you up some?)

A powerful air pump to suck air out of the microscope and form an airless space called a vacuum.

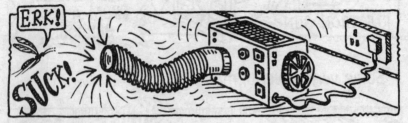

A wire and plug linked up to the electron gun.

Here's what you do…

1 Fix the electrode gun in the metal pipe so that it fires a beam of high energy electrons downwards and sweeps from side-to-side.

2 Below this, fix magnets on either side of the pipe. The magnetic forces direct the electrons into a narrow beam. Make sure the electron beam hits the place where the specimen is to be fixed and bounces on to the fluorescent screen. The screen should light up where it's hit by electrons.

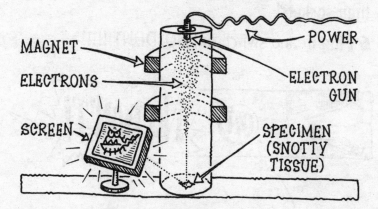

MAGNET

ELECTRONS

SCREEN

POWER

ELECTRON GUN

SPECIMEN (SNOTTY TISSUE)

3 Link the screen up to a computer that can interpret the hits on the screen as a picture of the specimen you'll be studying.

4 Use the pump to pump out the air from the tube. Atoms of air get in the way of the electrons and distort the picture.

5 Whoops! Silly me! Don't forget to place your specimen inside the machine. Actually this should be step **4** because if you put your hand in the airless tube your fingers could be wrenched out of their sockets!

6 Plug in and switch on! NO, DONT!!!!!!

An important announcement…

BET YOU NEVER KNEW!

1 Electron microscopes can create images of atoms. A scanning tunnelling electron microscope is a type of electron microscope that uses a tiny probe that fires electrons at the surface of an object. It has a device to pick up the electrons as they rebound to reveal the shapes of atoms.

2 The first scanning tunnelling electron microscope was built in 1981 by Swiss scientists Gerd Binnig and Heinrich Rohrer. Their first picture showed gold atoms that looked like an upside-down cardboard egg box. The scientists were awarded gold medals and the Nobel Prize (let's hope the medals didn't look like cardboard).

Meanwhile, back at the drawing board – here's how to build a microscope that's not quite so powerful as the electron microscope but it's easier to make and really very nice. You can use it to study this fascinating dead spider...

FASCINATING DEAD SPIDER

DARE YOU DISCOVER ... HOW TO BUILD YOUR OWN MICROSCOPE?

You will need:

a piece of card 2.5 cm wide by 5 cm long • a piece of cellophane (try using the clear wrapping from a greetings card) • scissors • sticky tape • a pencil or hole punch • a cardboard tube from a kitchen roll

What you do:

1 Use the hole punch or pencil point to make a hole 5 mm across in the centre of the card.

2 Cover the hole with cellophane and secure with sticky tape.

3 Cut a length of tube 5 cm long and then cut into it two slots 3 cm long and 2.5 cm apart coming down from one end. Lift up the cardboard between them to make a little window. Place the tube on top of the spider and place the card on top of the tube.

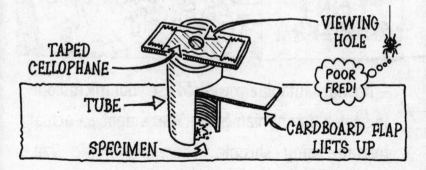

VIEWING HOLE

TAPED CELLOPHANE

POOR FRED!

TUBE →

TUBE

SPECIMEN

CARDBOARD FLAP LIFTS UP

4 Pick up a drop of water on the tip of the pencil and let it fall over the cellophane covering the hole. Make sure the drop covers the hole.

5 Hold your eye very close to the drop and look through it. You should see the spider's eight eyes and fangs in fascinating close up detail. Just don't let it give you nightmares afterwards…

THOSE EIGHT STARING EYES AND FEARSOME FANGS – I CAN'T SLEEP MUM!

Now just imagine you could use your microscope to spot a tiny human being. That's right an actual human being shrunk to a microscopic size. Impossible? Wait till you read this story…

IT'S A SMALL WORLD!

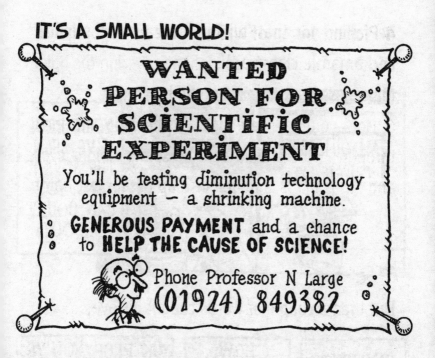

WANTED PERSON FOR SCIENTIFIC EXPERIMENT

You'll be testing diminution technology equipment – a shrinking machine.

GENEROUS PAYMENT and a chance to **HELP THE CAUSE OF SCIENCE!**

Phone Professor N Large
(01924) 849382

No one knew what to expect from the professor's new shrinking machine, but one thing was clear. The person who agreed to test it had to be ever so brave ... or ever so stupid. Only fearless private eye MI Gutzache had the experience for the job – and a very bad experience it was. And *no way* was he falling for that 'all for the cause of science' cockamamie clap-trap!

But then a couple of words caught his eye...

I wasn't going to volunteer for nothing but I needed the green backs. I figured I'd done it all and seen it all - but I hadn't seen nothing. I took the case and I should have known better. It was my first mistake.

I'm afraid none of my scientific colleagues wanted to volunteer for the test - they all muttered something about "unacceptable risk factors". I explained to Gutzache that the new machine was capable of shrinking a human to the size of a microbe!

SO YOU WON'T BE NEEDING THAT!

I heard the Prof but I didn't like what I was hearing. I wanted out but the Prof suggested a small test. "No risk," he said. But he was wrong and I was the fall guy. I stood under the machine as he switched it on. Just one tiny little test...

I placed a pin upright under the microscope but outside the shrinking ray for Gutzache to inspect and report on. It would be a fascinating opportunity to compare Gutzache's view with that of the microscope.

Gutzache felt the gentle warmth of the rays falling on him like summer sunshine. It didn't feel too bad until he noticed that he was shrinking. The pin beside him was getting bigger and bigger until it looked like a giant column. There were ridges and furrows running down its sides and its top was no longer sharp and pointed but rounded like an enormous Christmas pudding.

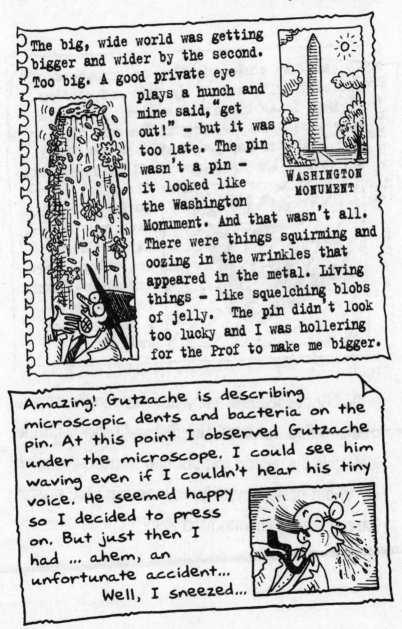

The big, wide world was getting bigger and wider by the second. Too big. A good private eye plays a hunch and mine said, "get out!" – but it was too late. The pin wasn't a pin – it looked like the Washington Monument. And that wasn't all. There were things squirming and oozing in the wrinkles that appeared in the metal. Living things – like squelching blobs of jelly. The pin didn't look too lucky and I was hollering for the Prof to make me bigger.

WASHINGTON MONUMENT

Amazing! Gutzache is describing microscopic dents and bacteria on the pin. At this point I observed Gutzache under the microscope. I could see him waving even if I couldn't hear his tiny voice. He seemed happy so I decided to press on. But just then I had ... ahem, an unfortunate accident...

Well, I sneezed...

59

It was like something blew up somewhere close. It blew me off my feet and sent me flying. I saw blobs all around, I figured they were snot. Getting in the way of a sneeze is bad for you – it sure was bad for me. Didn't the Prof know about handkerchiefs?

The floor looked hundreds of miles away and the only way was down. One thing I knew for sure – thanks to a sneeze ... I was gonna be crowbait.

Will Gutzache make a tiny little mess on the carpet? You can find out later! But first we'll stick with the detective theme and find out how microscopes solve small but messy mysteries ... including the sinister case of the treacherous toilet thief!

MICROSCOPIC DETECTIVE MYSTERIES

There's a whole branch of police work called forensic science that uses microscopes to search for clues to crimes. Here are some forensic clues that we've borrowed from a police museum.

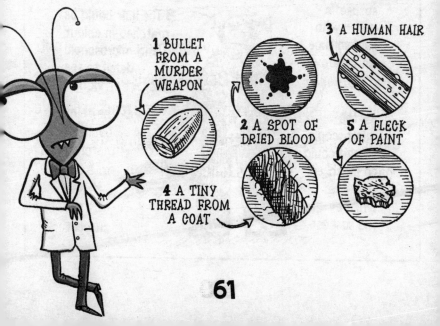

1 BULLET FROM A MURDER WEAPON

2 A SPOT OF DRIED BLOOD

3 A HUMAN HAIR

4 A TINY THREAD FROM A COAT

5 A FLECK OF PAINT

And here's how these clues can catch a villain…

Microscopic monsters fact file

Name: Forensic science

Basic facts: Forensic scientists check the scene of a crime for tiny clues.

1 Scratches on the side of the bullet might match grooves in the barrel of the suspect's gun – who said science isn't groovy?

2 Blood can be tested for DNA. This substance – known as deoxyribonucleic acid (de-oxy-ri-bo new-clay-ick acid) – forms a unique chemical code in all of us. If DNA from the victim is found on the murder suspect then chances are they did it.

3 The hair could be matched in colour and microscopic detail to the suspect or victim.

4 The microscopic thread could be matched to a coat worn by the suspect.

5 The paint could be matched to a car driven by the suspect.

Monstrous details: Some forensic evidence is very horrible indeed. Would you fancy looking through a microscope at a pool of sick left at a crime scene to find out the exact foods eaten by a suspect? It's all in a day's work for a forensic scientist!

SWEETCORN, MUSHROOMS AND . . . CATFOOD. INTERESTING!

So how would you measure up as a forensic scientist? Don't worry, there won't be any pools of sick to peer into. Just a true crime story of how the microscope helped to catch a ruthless thief ... with his trousers down. Can you help trap the suspect?

63

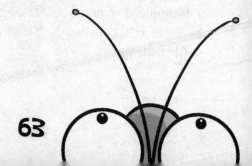

THE TREACHEROUS TOILET THIEF

Lyons, France 1922

"It's a disgrace!" grumbled the old woman. "My pension money is missing and someone in your post office has stolen it! I'm 86 years old and this sort of thing didn't happen when I was a girl! There ought to be a law against it!"

The postmaster looked harassed.

"There *is* a law, madam, and rest assured I will make it my business to catch the thief and return the money."

The old woman shuffled out still wagging her skinny finger and muttering complaints. When she had gone the postmaster took a deep breath and summoned his two most trusted staff. They were very different. Jean was small and wiry and Jacques was built like an extra-large pillar box. The postmaster looked sternly at the pair.

"That's the third complaint today. I am ordering you to catch the thief before he gets us into any more trouble. I have devised a cunning plan, but I am afraid it is rather unpleasant."

Jacques was so proud of winning his chief's confidence that he didn't notice the words, "rather unpleasant". He beamed self-importantly.

"That's all right boss, you can count on us for anything!"

"Very well," said the postmaster. "I believe that the thief is opening the letters and stealing the money in the toilet." And with that he outlined his plan.

By the time the two postmen left they were looking rather less happy.

Jean prodded his friend's bulging tummy. "You fat fool! Why did you tell him he could count on us? Now look what you've done!"

Jacques looked as if he was going to cry. "It wasn't my fault!" he moaned. "How was I to know we'd be spying on the toilets?"

"It's a terrible inconvenience!" continued Jean.

Jacques nodded gloomily. "I know it's terrible in them conveniences, but we could always wear clothes pegs on our noses."

"Oh, shut up!" snapped Jean.

By 11 the next morning the two postmen were very uncomfortable. They were cramped and doubled up in the roof space of the toilets. And they were sickened by the revolting sights they'd been subjected to as they spied through the eyeholes that had been drilled in the ceilings of the cubicles.

"How many have you seen?" whispered Jean.

"Oh, I haven't been counting – ten, maybe 12."

"Anyone do anything bad?"

Jacques giggled. "All of them. The last one in my cubicle must have eaten lots of beans – he was a real stinker! This investigation is getting up my nose."

But Jean put his finger to his lips.

"Shut up, Jacques, there's someone in the toilet!"

"Where's he going – yours or mine?"

"Mine. Ssh, Jacques – I think it's the thief!"

There was a ripping sound as envelopes were opened and a rustling as their contents were rifled and a crackle as postal orders and bank notes were hurriedly stuffed into the thief's pockets.

"I want a look!" cried Jacques shoving aside his friend. But his huge knee banged the floor sending a fine drizzle of plaster into the cubicle. The thief hastily unlocked the door and fled the toilet.

"Now look what you've done!" hissed Jean.

"It wasn't my fault!" said Jacques miserably. "How can I help it if the floor got in the way?!"

Back in the postmaster's office the boss was drumming his fingers on the table.

"Well, what did he look like?" he asked the two postmen.

"He wore a cap," said Jacques.

The postmaster gave him a dirty look. "You fool, all postmen wear a cap – it's one of our regulations. Is that it? So all we've got is a damaged toilet roof and nothing to go on!"

Jacques whispered, "Does he mean that no one can go to the toilet?" and Jean gave him a kick.

"What was that?" said the postmaster sharply.

"Jacques said the thief might still have the envelopes on him." said Jean.

"You fool!" snapped the postmaster. "The thief is not stupid. The first thing he'll have done is to throw them away. Are you sure you didn't see anything else – any tiny clues. You'd better think of something or I'll have you watching the toilets for the next six months!"

Jean shuffled his feet unhappily. "Chief, it's not our fault! I mean – we don't have microscopes for eyes!" he said.

Suddenly the postmaster thumped his desk, making the two postmen jump.

"Microscopes!" he cried excitedly. "Of course – that's it!"

Police scientist Edmond Locard was middle-aged and neatly dressed and looked like a mild-mannered bank manager. As he listened to the postmaster's story, he stroked his moustache and placed the tips of his fingers together – showing off his clean, neatly trimmed fingernails.

"Hmm," he said. "A fascinating case. We'll need all the postmen's coats for microscopic laboratory analysis."

A few days later Locard was staring down the eyepiece of his microscope at the crucial evidence. His face betrayed no excitement as he adjusted the focus knob. Then he made a few neatly scripted notes in his tiny handwriting.

After examining the evidence make a very interesting discovery. Sometimes it is a mistake by an innocent party that leads to the solution of the crime. A thorough investigation was carried out. Every worker at the Post Office ... notes have been taken with

What vital clue had Locard spotted?

a) Germs that the thief picked up in the toilet.

b) Threads on the thief's coat that matched threads found in the toilet.

c) Tiny bits of plaster from the ceiling.

d) Tiny fibres of paper from the envelopes.

ANSWER

c) The thief had brushed his coat but there were microscopic specks of plaster still on it. If there were germs from the toilet these could have been picked up by any of the postmen, and, since all the postmen wore the same type of coat, the threads would not have identified the thief. Paper fibres might have proved that the thief handled the envelopes but not that he had stolen the money.

COULD YOU BE A FORENSIC DETECTIVE?

Don't worry! You don't have to spy on the school toilets! Here's an easy experiment to do instead...

DARE YOU DISCOVER ... HOW TO COLLECT FIBRES?

You will need:

• a piece of sticky tape

What you do:

Press the sticky tape firmly on the carpet and then lift it up.

What do you notice?

ANSWER

The tape is covered with carpet fibres which you can examine with your microscope. If you're lucky, you'll find a few human hairs or hairs from the dog or cat. This technique is used by forensic scientists to collect fibres from a crime scene. If they're found on the clothes of a suspect then this could link the suspect with the crime.

THE PANTS OF PERIL

Here are samples of polyester and cotton cut from two pairs of underpants. Look identical, don't they? Well, let's peer through the microscope, if we dare...

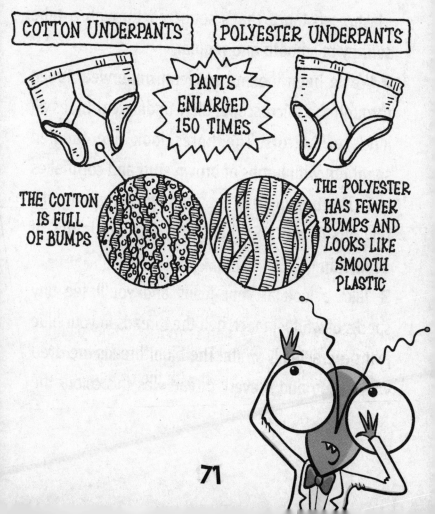

COTTON UNDERPANTS

POLYESTER UNDERPANTS

PANTS ENLARGED 150 TIMES

THE COTTON IS FULL OF BUMPS

THE POLYESTER HAS FEWER BUMPS AND LOOKS LIKE SMOOTH PLASTIC

FOUL FIBRE FACTS

1 Cotton fibres come from the outer layer of seed cases on the cotton plant and they're never perfectly smooth. Polyester fibres begin life as a plastic substance that's squeezed through a tube so they're smooth and regular.

2 We've been looking at clean underwear. Seen through the microscope, dirty underwear hides all kinds of horrors. The fibres look like tangled spaghetti with lumps of brown stuff and cornflakes in it. The brown stuff is ... no, you're wrong, it's tiny bits of dirt and the 'cornflakes' are lumps of dead skin.

3 Take a look at your jeans and you'll see tiny specks of white. In fact, half the threads in your blue jeans are actually white! The blue threads are dyed with indigo and if every thread was this colour the jeans would be bright blue. The white threads give the jeans a 'washed 'n' faded' appearance.

4 Wool comes from sheep. Oh, so you knew that? Well, stop bleating – the fibres in wool are sheep hair and, like your own hair, they're made of a substance called keratin. Enlarged 1,000 times through a microscope you can see tiny scales of hair like shiny crazy paving.

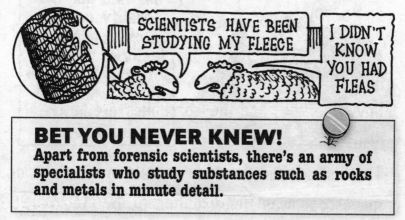

SCIENTISTS HAVE BEEN STUDYING MY FLEECE

I DIDN'T KNOW YOU HAD FLEAS

BET YOU NEVER KNEW!
Apart from forensic scientists, there's an army of specialists who study substances such as rocks and metals in minute detail.

Now, you might think that anyone who wants to look closely at boring things like rocks and metals is the sort of person who is called Norman and wears an anorak and very thick glasses. And of course, you'd be right.

Here's Norman to explain his hobby…

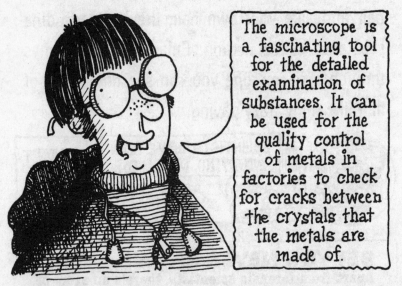

The microscope is a fascinating tool for the detailed examination of substances. It can be used for the quality control of metals in factories to check for cracks between the crystals that the metals are made of.

The first scientist to study crystals in metals using a microscope was Henry Clifton Sorby (1826–1908). He sounds a bit like Norman – after all, his idea of a fun holiday was to sail his yacht up and down the coast studying how the tides move lumps of sewage that have been flushed into rivers. (He did this for a British Government Committee on the River Thames.) But he must have been a clever person because he taught himself science, and he once said his aim was…

…not to pass an examination but to qualify myself for a course for original investigation

Are you brave enough to quote this to your teacher?

In fact, microscopic investigation of materials can be very exciting – as you're about to find out…

EXCITING MATERIALS QUIZ

Here are some exciting jobs that require a microscope. And just to make the quiz even more interesting, we've added a job for which the microscope is about as sensible as a pair of exploding underpants — can you spot it?

1 Looking for the causes of a plane crash.

2 Studying rocks at the bottom of the sea.

3 Checking the quality of diamonds.

4 Looking at gold to make sure that it's 100 per cent gold and not mixed with some cheaper metal.

LEAD'S PUT IT THIS WAY, MR SILVER, YOU'LL BE BRASSED OFF WITH MY FINDINGS AND YOU MAY WANT TO CALL THE COPPERS.

ANSWERS
2 It's hard to use a microscope underwater and at the bottom of the sea there isn't enough light to see anything. It would be better to take a bit of rock to the surface and study it there.
All the rest are TRUE...
1 Accident investigators often look at metal from wrecked planes to find cracks and the marks made by strains just before the accident. These might help explain why the accident happened.

3 The microscope shows how well the diamond has been cut. By the way, if you can't afford diamonds you could study salt grains. Each is a single box-like crystal about 60 micrometres square. But do this at mealtimes and you could be a-salted by your parents.

4 Like any metal, gold is made up of crystals a few micrometres wide that look like crazy paving. By looking at the shape of the crystals you can tell which are gold and which are junk.

But come to think of it, there are even more scientists who use microscopes. A microscope is pretty essential for scientists who study miniature lifeforms like putrid little plants and extra small (but still revolting) bugs. They might be small, but they make up for it in the horrible habits department.

Are you ready to uncover their slimy little secrets?

TINY TERRORS

Somebody had to be the first person to make an in-depth microscopic study of plants and bugs and that somebody happened to be a mistrustful, selfish and jealous man. Well, that's how his friends described him ... his enemies were a little more unkind.

Hall of fame: Robert Hooke (1635–1703)
Nationality: British

Robert was supposedly ugly inside and out and his hobby was spreading ugly rumours about people he didn't like, such as mega-star scientist Isaac Newton (1642–1727).

NEWTON? PAH! THE MAN'S A BUFFOON. YOU'D NEED ONE OF MY MICROSCOPES TO CHECK IF HE'S GOT A BRAIN AT ALL! AND THAT RIDICULOUS FALLING APPLE THEORY, BLAH, BLAH, DRONE, WITTER, ETC. ETC.

But Hooke was also a brilliant scientist who built his own microscope and published a book called *Micrographia* full of stomach-turning pictures of his discoveries. As you might expect, our old pal Leeuwenhoek was a big fan of this book and, although he couldn't read the English words, he enjoyed looking at the pictures. And now for a remarkable Horrible Science exclusive. Here is Robert Hooke in person! He's been dug up and brought back from the dead to tell us all about his discoveries...

DEAD BRAINY: ROBERT HOOKE

Is that the time? How long have I been dead?

Ah! here is my pride and joy — my microscope. Yes, you are allowed to gasp at my skill and cunning workmanship — it's all my own work you know!

OH GET ON WITH IT!

Sorry readers, RH was an extremely conceited and self-important person.

The light is provided by this oil lamp and this glass ball brightens the light and focuses it on the viewing platform on which I have placed the specimen.

OIL
FLAME
GLASS BALL
LENS
LENS POINTING AT SPECIMEN

Actually the lenses Hooke used were not as good as Leeuwenhoek's and he missed out on some of the things the Dutch scientist spotted.

I peer through the eyepiece of the microscope like so.

Using my microscope I looked at fungi (that's more than one fungus) and snowflakes. Those snowflakes were hard to see because they kept melting so I had to sit out in the cold with my microscope. It was snow joke, I can tell you!

SNOWFLAKE

FUNGI

One day I was looking at cork. Cork is a type of wood and I saw little boxes. Well, I called them "cells". It was a corker of a discovery — if I say so myself!

I was especially interested in plants. I looked at a stinging nettle and saw it had tiny hairs on its leaves. 'Hair's a mystery!' I thought — what are they for?

I touched a hair under the microscope and saw the end stick in my skin and poison run into my finger. I was stung into action I can tell you! Let's try it again...

OUCH — MY HAND! I WISH I WAS DEAD!

Hooke didn't actually understand what cells are for and how they worked (you can find out on page 147) but discovering them was still a great achievement. Later on we'll find out how Hooke studied bugs, but for the moment let's stick with those fungi and nasty little green plants. Oh yes, I'm afraid we have to...

Microscopic monsters fact file

Name: Fungi and tiny plants

Basic facts: We're talking about...

1 Fungi – aren't plants. They include moulds and yeasts.

2 Algae – including the green, slimy stuff that you find in ponds.

3 Lichens – actually a partnership between fungi and algae. Often found in tough places like Antarctica – fancy going there for a summer holiday?

Monstrous details: Algae thrive in water filled with sewage. And this is one of their nicer habits...

WANT TO CREATE YOUR OWN ALGAE FARM? DON'T FLUSH THE LOO FOR SIX MONTHS!

CUTE LITTLE ALGAE?

Some scientists think that algae have their charms, especially the microscopic algae that look like living balls of slime under a microscope. We decided to take them at their word and open up the world's first pet shop for algae...

ALGAE-PALS PET SHOP

SLITHER! SPLIT! SLITHER! SPLIT!

Are you a lonely scientist? Are you seeking a little friend, someone who will listen to your latest scientific theories without falling asleep? Look no further! To order – give us a ring and give us your money!

···🌸·· WARNING! ··🌸 ···

Algae breed by splitting in half. You might need to get some other micro creatures to eat your pets before they form a vast, slimy mass that poisons their water ... and *you* if you fall in!

A QUICK NOTE...
Yes, I know the word "pet" normally means a cute, furry animal but when you've got "plants" that swim around under their own steam, the distinction gets a little blurred.

1 Cute ceratium (ser-rat-tee-um)

Description: Looks like a homemade Christmas decoration that's gone wrong.

CHEERS!

Size: 0.5 mm

Cute features: Dagger-like spikes for protection from other microscopic creatures.

Feeding: Don't worry about feeding them – they use sunlight and carbon dioxide gas in the air to make sugar for food – a process called photosynthesis (as if you didn't know!).

Note: you can use your pet as a thermometer. The warmer the water, the more they stick their spikes out. This can be useful for working out if your bath is the right temperature!

2 Delightful diatoms
Description: Indescribable – pretty aren't they?

Size: 0.2 mm

Delightful features: They shine in the light because they have see-through bodies and hard box-like outer bodies that contain silica, which also makes up sand and glass.

Feeding: Photosynthesis.

To stop your pets multiplying too much, why not use an animal that looks like a plant? It's wild and wacky…

3 Hungry hydra

Description: A green rubber glove.

Size: 1.25 cm

Cute features: Stinging threads in its 'fingers' kill anything that comes near. Er, that's not too cute, is it?

Feeding: 'Fingers' grab the prey and bring it into the creature's mouth.

FOUL FUNGAL FEEDING

So you're anti-algae? Oh well, perhaps you'll be fungi-friendly? Enlarged over 500 times through a microscope, fungi look like trendy worms with Afro haircuts. But their eating habits are less pretty – as you're about to find out…

THE FUNGI GUIDE TO ETIQUETTE

by Madame Mould

IF YOU DESIRE TO BE ACCEPTED IN THE BEST HOUSES THEN ETIQUETTE IS ESSENTIAL – SO MIND YOUR MANNERS, MOULDS!

TABLE MANNERS

Eating is very important for fungi – so make sure you eat as much as you can whenever you can. (It's acceptable to burp gas afterwards.)

MUNCH! NIBBLE! SCOFF! CHEW! BURP!

BURP!

Four things not to do
NEVER...
- Ask permission before eating.
- Say, "please" or "thank you".
- Ask for a second helping – just help yourself anyway.
- Leave the table (before you've eaten it).

Two things to do
ALWAYS...

- Be prepared to eat anything – glue in wallpaper, metal in paints, wood, plaster. Fussy fungi are considered ill-mannered.

- Tell bacteria to back off. A good way to do this is to spray out substances that kill most bacteria like carbon dioxide or hydrogen cyanide. Yes, KILL THEM! I am sure that your hosts will approve of your thoughtfulness!

FOUL FUNGUS FACTS

1 Dry rot fungus will eat all the wooden bits in your house. It starts by growing in damp areas and extends its feeding tubes into dry areas of walls and floors! The only way to stop it is to cut out huge chunks of your home.

2 A fungus will push anything aside. Its feeding tubes are armoured with chitin, the tough stuff that protects insect bodies and makes beetles so hard to squash.

A TOUGH MATERIAL STOPS US GETTING SQUASHED...

IT'S CHITIN!

WHAT D'YOU MEAN, CHEATING? IT'S NOT A FLAMIN' GAME!!

3 Fungi only make small amounts of poisons and they don't harm humans – usually. But before the 1920s the deadly poison arsenic was often added to paints. Fungi ate the paints and sprayed out arsenic gas that smelt of garlic, and some people died.

Sounds fascinating? Well, your rotten spoilsport family will probably stop you breeding deadly fungi or dry rot in your bedroom. Never mind, why not use your microscope to study bugs instead? The rest of this chapter is about really tiny bugs that you can only get a good look at through the microscope. These bugs ain't going to win any beauty contests and their habits are equally repulsive … are *you* ready to face the ugly truth?

BUGS BEHAVING BADLY 1: TAKING A RIDE WITHOUT PAYING

1 Many bugs have smaller bugs less than 0.2 mm long that live on them. Bee mites hang on to … well, what do you think they hang on to…?

I LIKE IT HERE

YEAH, IT'S THE BEE'S KNEES!

They don't do any harm, so I guess they just think it's a nice place to bee and it gives them a buzz.

2 Feather mites live on birds. There's a type of Mexican parrot that has 30 varieties of feather mite. The mites eat bits of worn feather and dead skin, and if they overeat they probably feel sick as a parrot.

3 A pseudoscorpion hitches lifts on a fly's hairs. If it gets bored of the high life, it brings the fly down to earth with a nasty nip of its poison claws and eats its body!

So you're not afraid to see a pseudoscorpion up close? Well, here's something for you to get your claws into... Who said science wasn't down to earth?

SINISTER SOIL CREATURES

Soil is crawling with bugs, but thanks to the microscope you don't have to stick your nose in the flower bed to spot them up close.

Here are menacing microscope views of two common bugs. I've added some labels to explain what their horrible little body bits are for...

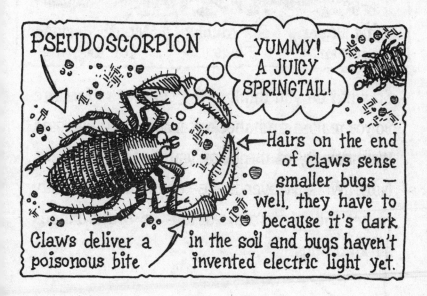

The pseudoscorpions eat springtails. (Yes, they really do have springs in their tails and if they were bigger they'd win the world pogo-jumping contest!)

SPRINGTAIL

ARGH! AN EVIL PSEUDOSCORPION!

Spring under abdomen

Six stubby legs

Mouth designed for chewing

So what do you think of the chapter so far? Are you appalled and shocked by the ugliness and the brutality of the bugs featured? You will be. Now here's a never-to-be-repeated opportunity to get the microscopic details on brutal blood-sucking bugs.

BUGS BEHAVING BADLY 2:
SUCKING BLOOD

Forget vampires – some bugs make Count Dracula look like a vegetarian – as you can find out by studying them through the microscope.

1 Take fleas for example…

Many types of animal have their own special type of flea – dog fleas on dogs, armadillo fleas on armadillos, hedgehog fleas on … oh well, I expect you get the point. Oddly enough, hedgehog fleas have their own passengers. Tiny mites hide under their scales. I expect they enjoy life at the sharp end.

2 Flea babies are too small to suck blood but they don't lose out. They eat their parents' poo, which is rich in digested blood. It makes supper time less of a chore for the parents, but would you really want to eat your dad's poop?

3 One type of flea is called a jigger. It lays its eggs between a person's toes. As it digs a pit in the skin in which to lays its eggs, the female sucks the victim's blood and can introduce germs which cause blood poisoning. I expect the victim says, "Well, I be jiggered!"

BET YOU NEVER KNEW!
1 Three hundred years ago, people wore special flea traps round their necks. Each trap was a container with holes for the fleas to creep into and a little sticky rod to ensure they didn't creep out again. Queen Kristina of Sweden (1626–1689) invented an alternative method – she blasted the fleas with a tiny 10-cm cannon.

2 Wacky Victorian scientist Frank Buckland actually liked fleas. He spent 20 years learning how to train them to do tricks and even made a model ship for them to pull. He used to feed his pets each night with a refreshing drop of his own blood.

A LOUSY EXPERIMENT

Our long dead pal Robert Hooke did another revolting experiment with another blood-sucking bug – a louse. Through his microscope he watched a louse sucking blood from his hand into its see-through body. He said:

SUCK!

I could plainly see a small current of blood which came from its snout and poured directly into its belly.

I expect the louse was wondering why this funny man was staring at him over lunch.

BET YOU NEVER KNEW!

1 In one ancient Swedish town a louse chose the mayor. The candidates laid their beards on a table in front of a louse. The owner of the beard chosen by the louse to live in was declared mayor. It sounds a really lousy election.

2 Lice sometimes carry rickettsia (things a bit like bacteria) that live in their bodies and come out in their poo. If a human scratches lice poo into their lice bites, the rickettsia get into the body and cause the deadly disease typhus.

And by some revolting coincidence we're going to be meeting some murderous microbes in the next chapter. Did I say, "coincidence"? Oh well, it's a small world...

MURDEROUS MICROBES

Imagine everything became invisible and the microbes currently invisible began to glow. Everything – trees, houses, people, school dinner and dogs' poo would disappear. But you could still see where they were because the outlines of these objects and almost everything else would be picked out in ghostly glowing microbes. Yes, I'm afraid everything is CRAWLING with the little monsters!

Microscopic monsters fact file

Name: Microbes

Basic facts: Microbes include bacteria (plus similar lifeforms called archaea), protists and viruses.

1 Bacteria – see next page.

2 Some protists change their body shape as they move and engulf bacteria. So if you're tiny don't ask one to come "round" for lunch.

3 Viruses are even smaller so you'll need an electron microscope to spot one. They're basically bundles of DNA (and if you DNA know what I'm talking about turn back to page 62 to refresh your memory).

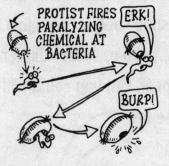

PROTIST FIRES PARALYZING CHEMICAL AT BACTERIA

ERK!

BURP!

Monstrous details: All three can cause deadly diseases.

1 Bacteria cause diseases such as the plague and the lung disease TB.

2 Protists cause malaria – a killer disease which is spread by mosquitoes.

3 Viruses cause disease by breaking into cells and forcing them to make new viruses until the cells die of exhaustion. Diseases caused by viruses include yellow fever and flu.

FLU VIRUS
Attacks cells in the throat (can be a pain in the neck).

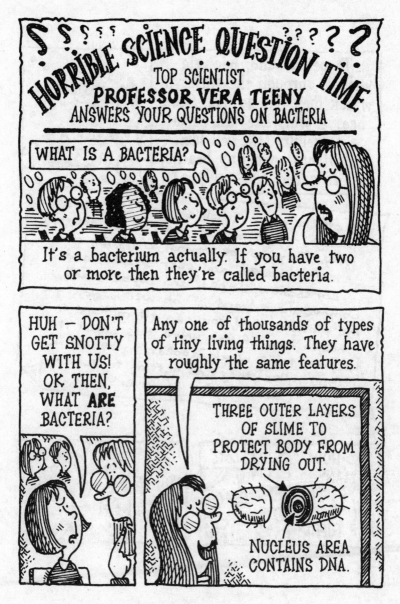

HORRIBLE SCIENCE QUESTION TIME

TOP SCIENTIST
PROFESSOR VERA TEENY
ANSWERS YOUR QUESTIONS ON BACTERIA

WHAT IS A BACTERIA?

It's a bacterium actually. If you have two or more then they're called bacteria.

HUH — DON'T GET SNOTTY WITH US! OK THEN, WHAT **ARE** BACTERIA?

Any one of thousands of types of tiny living things. They have roughly the same features.

THREE OUTER LAYERS OF SLIME TO PROTECT BODY FROM DRYING OUT.

NUCLEUS AREA CONTAINS DNA.

101

To get around, bacteria wriggle through the water in which they like to live. Some beat a whip-like tail called a flagellum (fla-gell-lum) and others have tiny beating hairs called cilia (silly-a).

WRIGGLE!

BEAT!

Bacteria come in all shapes and sizes - though, to be honest, they're all pretty tiny. They can be round, and thin, and lemon-shaped, and pear-shaped, and corkscrew-shaped, and square, and comma-shaped and ... oh well ... you get the picture. And you can fit millions in a match box. If you were this small the kitchen table would appear to be 640 km (400 miles) long and getting to school would take for ever!

SO HOW MANY TYPES OF BACTERIA ARE THERE?

Lots

CAN YOU BE MORE EXACT?

No

Scientists from the University of Southern California found 61 types of bacteria living in a hot spring in Yellowstone National Park. 57 were unknown to science. Some scientists think that every pinch of soil could contain 10,000 different types of bacteria but they haven't got round to counting them all yet.

Any volunteers to count them?

Although, we're talking awfully big numbers. An average-sized lawn holds countless billions of individual bacteria — about 4.5 kg by weight.

And they're eaten by an army of tiny creatures such as protists and slimy nematode worms with no eyes and six rubbery lips

WHERE ELSE DO BACTERIA LIVE?

SO WHAT DO BACTERIA DO ALL DAY?

Where don't they live! Most bacteria live in 'cities' of slime in massive piles like tower blocks 200 micrometres high (that's BIG by their standards). Favourite places for slime cities are — are you ready for this? — sewage pipes, false teeth, contact lenses, the guts and just about anywhere else you can imagine...

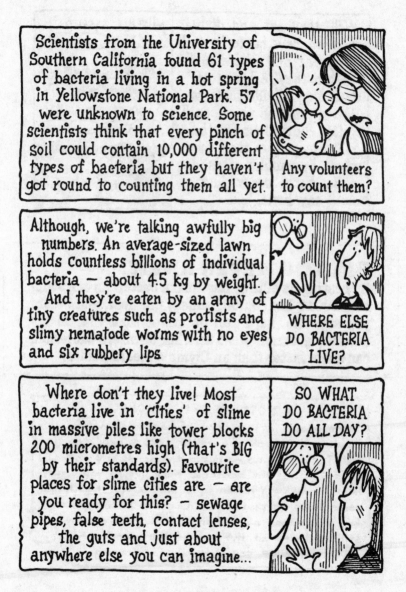

Well, they eat and divide to make new bacteria and they eat and divide and when they're bored of that they divide and eat. Well, I suppose they could play football under the microscope but then they might be caught off-slide! Ha, ha — sorry, just my little joke.

BET YOU NEVER KNEW!

By beating its cilia or flagellum a bacterium can swim at 0.00016 km (0.0001 miles) per hour, and before you say, "Ha, ha, I can do faster than that in my swimming lesson." Read this. For its size, a bacterium can swim faster than an Olympic record holder!

A NOTE TO THE READER...

Some people are scared of bacteria. After reading this book you might feel scared, too. DON'T. Most do us no harm and some are actually good for us: the bacteria that live in your gut help to make Vitamin K, a substance that helps your blood to clot. Bacteria have been around for thousands of millions of years and they'll still be there at the end of the world. And anyway, they're scientifically fascinating!

Bacteria might be tiny – but they're TOUGH. Their secret is to form spores. These are thick capsules that protect their bodies and they can live for years. You might be surprised to learn that bacteria have really boastful personalities and love bragging about their survival feats. OK, I just made that bit up but just imagine they *were* like this…

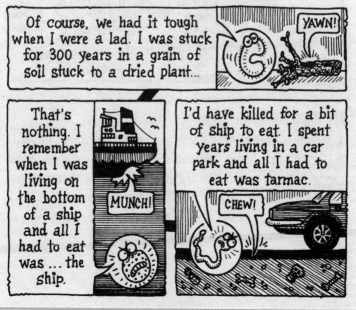

BOASTFUL BACTERIA

Of course, we had it tough when I were a lad. I was stuck for 300 years in a grain of soil stuck to a dried plant…

YAWN!

That's nothing. I remember when I was living on the bottom of a ship and all I had to eat was … the ship.

MUNCH!

I'd have killed for a bit of ship to eat. I spent years living in a car park and all I had to eat was tarmac.

CHEW!

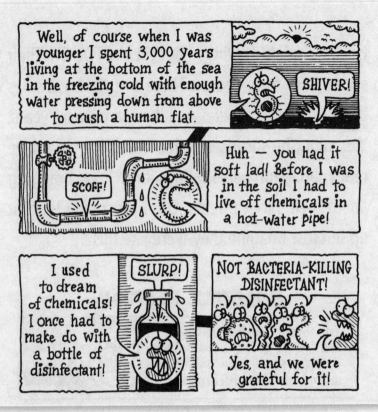

ALL these boasts are TRUE!

1 Scientists have revived bacteria on plant specimens this old.

2 Bacteria that live in polluted sea water can eat ships! What happens is bacteria in the water eat sulphur and turn it into sulphide. This joins to iron atoms on the ship to make a black smelly chemical called iron sulphide. Other bacteria happily guzzle this foul mixture – and eat the ship.

3 It's true – some bacteria eat tarmac. Mind you, it takes them hundreds of years to do it – it's a bit like you trying to eat a pile of hamburgers the size of Mount Everest!

4 Bacteria live at the bottom of the sea. But they're so used to the pressure of the water that when they are brought up to the surface where there's less water crushing down on them, their little bodies go pop.

5 Some bacteria make themselves at home in your hot-water pipes. They feed off chemicals in the water called sulphates and make hydrogen sulphide. This stinky substance dissolves your pipes and makes your water pong of rotten eggs.

6 Disinfectant contains a chemical called phenol that kills most bacteria – but some bacteria think it's a treat and happily guzzle it!

BET YOU NEVER KNEW!

1 When bacteria feed inside a dead body, the methane gas they give off makes the body swell up to three times its size. There have even been cases of dead bodies blowing up. It's said that this supposedly happened to King Henry VIII's corpse. Yuck!

2 Methane is also made inside cows by bacteria that live in the cow's stomach and digest the tough cell walls of grass. The cow can then digest the grass more easily. Cows get rid of the methane in huge burps or farts. The cows don't mean to be rude but there's no udder choice.

MICROSCOPIC EXPRESSIONS

A scientist says:

I COLLECT AUTOTROPHS

Do you say....?

COOL!
I COLLECT
AUTOGRAPHS
TOO!

ANSWER

No. He said *autotrophs* – and if you don't know what they are, keep reading! It's a posh term for being able to make food from simple chemicals – and no, we're not talking cookery lessons here. Autotrophs include plants and certain bacteria that make their food using photosynthesis. (Remember that word? It's on page 85.) Other autotrophic bacteria feed off chemicals such as sulphur, as you've just found out...

BACTERIA BREAKFAST QUIZ

Which of these 'foods' would bacteria NOT fancy for breakfast…?
a) Your mum's bottle of vitamin C pills.
b) A bucket of sulphuric acid.
c) An old pair of welly boots.
d) An ancient temple.

ANSWERS
a) For some reason bacteria don't eat vitamin C. Maybe they don't like healthy foods? b) Some bacteria live happily in weak sulphuric acid and can even eat it! c) Bacteria happily scoff latex — a kind of tree gum that is the raw material of rubber. During the Second World War many homes burnt down in air raids because bacteria had eaten holes in the fire hoses. The rubber in welly boots is treated with sulphur but as you know, some bacteria can eat this chemical. d) Angkor in Cambodia is one of the wonders of the world.

It's also a giant bacteria snack bar. Bacteria in the soil are making sulphide, which is drawn up with moisture into the stones of the temple. More bacteria eat the chemical and poo out an acid that eats away the temple.

COULD YOU BE A SCIENTIST?

The landlord of a bar in the Yukon, Canada offered his guests a disgusting cocktail. It was champagne … with a human toe in it complete with toenail. (The toe had been found in a log cabin — no one knew what it was doing there but I expect it was trying to find its feet.) Anyway, the landlord challenged his customers to drink the concoction saying:

You can drink it fast, you can drink it slow — but the lips have got to touch the toe!

ARGH!

But why didn't bacteria eat the toe and make it rot?
a) It was too revolting even for bacteria.
b) It was so cold in the Yukon that the bacteria froze.
c) The toe had been pickled in alcohol and few bacteria can live in these conditions.

ANSWER
c) You'll be interested to know that 725 people actually drank the disgusting drink but in 1980 someone accidentally swallowed the toe. I guess that was just toe bad.

TEACHER'S TEA-BREAK TEASER
Arm yourself with this treacherously
tricky teaser and a pencil and
terrorize your teacher's tea-break.
Beat out a little tune on the
staffroom door. When it opens smile
an angelic smile and ask:

ANSWER

Told you this teaser's treacherous! The answer
isn't, "yes" or "no", but, "half of it". Bacteria will
happily eat the wooden bit but the 'lead' is
actually baked clay and graphite (a form of pure
carbon). Bacteria can't eat this and that's the
reason why bacteria don't eat diamonds either
because they're made of pure carbon, too.

STINKY SHOES

An old pair of shoes is home
to millions of microscopic
monsters. Here's a tiny circle
of old shoe leather.

And here's what it looks like through the
microscope. Don't be shy, take a peek. Oh, that's
GROSS! The leather looks like crazy paving and
the tiny life forms look crazy, too. They think your
old shoes are a cheesy snack! They certainly smell
like one.

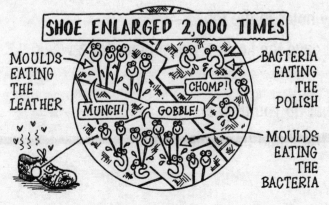

SHOE ENLARGED 2,000 TIMES

MOULDS EATING THE LEATHER

MUNCH!

CHOMP!

GOBBLE!

BACTERIA EATING THE POLISH

MOULDS EATING THE BACTERIA

DARE YOU DISCOVER ... HOW TO PROVIDE A SNUG, COSY HOME FOR BACTERIA?

You will need:

- a jar filled with water
- some grass and a pair of scissors
- adult to handle the scissors
- cling film and a pin

What you do:

1 Order the adult to cut the grass into pieces and add it to the water.

2 Cover with cling film and use the pin to make tiny holes in the top.

3 Leave the jar in a warm place for a week.

What do you notice?

a) The liquid has gone cloudy.

b) The liquid has gone green.

c) The liquid has gone frothy and orange and is escaping from the jar and eating everything in sight.

ANSWER

a) The cloudiness is made by millions of bacteria happily eating the grass. The bacteria were on the grass and in the air before you sealed the jar. Empty the jar outside and ask a grown-up to wash it with disinfectant. If **c)** then CONGRATULATIONS, you've discovered a new form of bacteria!

Anyway, we're going to tear ourselves away from the slimy world of bacteria now. Don't worry, they'll plop up pretty nastily in the next chapter. But right now we're moving on to the equally slimy world of protists.

PROWLING PROTISTS

The first person to spot protists under the microscope (they're too small to see any other way) was our old pal Leeuwenhoek. Wanna know what he saw? Here's what a protist looks like. Fancy finding that on your cornflakes?

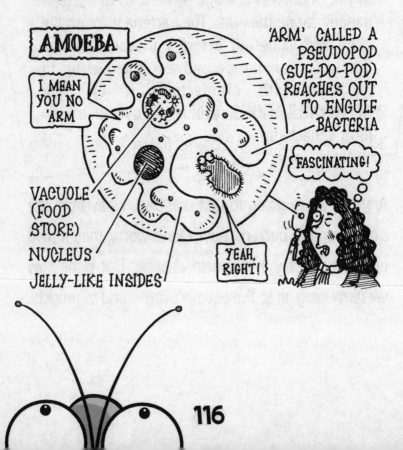

DARE YOU DISCOVER ... HOW TO MAKE AN AMOEBA?

You will need:

• a paper hankie (not a snotty one)

What you do:

1 Make two tears 4 cm long in each side of the hankie. (This will help to make an amoeba-like shape in the water.)

2 Screw the hankie up tightly.

3 Twist any sticking out points of hankie into points to make an amoeba shape.

4 Put it in water. If you stir the water around your amoeba will appear to move. BEWARE, it might engulf your finger! And if you find that hard to swallow read this...

BET YOU NEVER KNEW!

Protists can breed very fast. For example, a paramecium (pa-ra-me-see-um) divides every 22 hours. If one started splitting on New Year's Day, by 7 March it would have formed a huge slimy ball 1.6 km across. Little more than a month later it would have grown to the size of the Earth! Fortunately, other tiny creatures are public-spirited enough to eat the paramecium before it takes over the world!

AN URGENT NOTE TO THE READER...

Do you walk on the grass? Well, don't. IF YOU WALK ON THE GRASS MILLIONS OF INNOCENT TINY CREATURES WILL DIE!!!! Your feet squash the soil and push moisture out of it and this causes the slime moulds to appear!

"So what's a slime mould?" I hear you ask nervously. Well, don't feel too anxious – slime moulds are harmless to humans and you probably didn't eat one in your school dinner the other day. But if you're still curious, this slime mould's autobiography should answer all your questions...

MY LIFE AS A SLIME MOULD

By A Meeba
Published by Slimy & Creep

I don't remember when I was born because I was very young at the time. But I was certainly an amoeba - I only became part of a slime mould later on. I loved playing in the dark, murky soil - well, it's where my roots are! And although I didn't have too many friends there were always bacteria to keep me company - until I gobbled them up!

One day a kid walked over the lawn. I felt a huge rumble and a crash and a shaking and the soil became so dry that the bacteria stopped dividing. Soon my vacuole was rumbling. Then I saw another amoeba. This amoeba made a chemical signal and I felt drawn to follow it. And soon there was another amoeba following me and before I knew it I was part of a long line of amoebas "Oh goodie!" I thought. "Let's go line dancing!"

Soon we were flowing together (still under the ground, of course). So I just went with the flow until we oozed into a slug shape. "Wow!" I thought. "I've always wanted to be a gastropod!"

Editor's note: This formation is actually called a "slug" and it's a form of slime-mould.

Editor's note: That's the posh name for a slug.

We crept onwards. Behind us was a glistening trail of

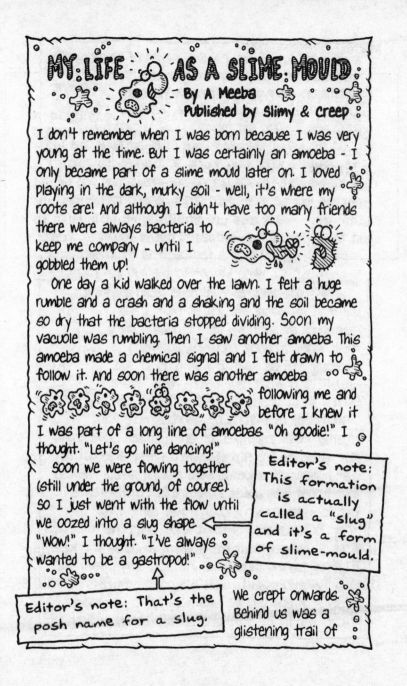

119

slime made out of the jelly-like insides of amoebas
that had been trampled in the rush and ripped
to bits on sharp grains of earth. What an
heroic sacrifice - those amoebas really had
guts! Well, I could see them!

On the way I chatted to the other amoebas and
they said the world was ending. So I asked the others
where we were heading but no one knew. Then one old
amoeba mumbled something about heading to the light
and heat - or did she say we were going
for a light eat? I'd have happily
murdered a few bacteria for breakfast!
When we got to the surface I was
gob-smacked - I'd never seen anything
like it in my entire life. (Oh, all right, I hadn't
seen much at all in my life!) It was a slimy
tower made of living, squishing, squirming
amoebas! It was vast, it was huge, IT WAS
GIGANTIC! It must have been - hmm, let me
think - all of one-tenth of a millimetre high!

Thousands of millions of amoebas were piling
together higher and higher. Groaning noises came from
deep inside the pile and wild rumours flew amongst us
that millions of amoebas were making a hard chemical
that turned their bodies stiff and killing themselves
just to make sure our lovely tower didn't topple over!

I started climbing. Higher and higher I
crawled, past the groaning amoebas who were
turning themselves into hard lumps, past the
amoebas who were holding up countless
others. Call me ambitious but I just had to
get to the top! As I climbed I noticed that I

too was changing. My body was becoming hard and tough. "OOPS!" I thought, "It's tough at the top." But no, I was growing a capsule. A space capsule to protect my body. Then I was on top of the tower and I felt the wind. A breath of air blew me away and all I remember was a buffeting on my capsule - but I'd escaped the end of the world! I was shaking like a bag of jelly! (Well, maybe that's because I am a bag of jelly?)

Eventually I landed in this nice damp bit of earth with plenty of bacteria. But I was lucky - 99.9 per cent of the amoebas didn't make it. I might be a humble amoeba but I'm a survivor and that makes me a bit special, in my own small way...

THE END

SCIENTIFIC NOTE...
And all this happens because YOU walked on the grass! Scientists aren't too sure of the details but amoebas form slime moulds in dry conditions. The process is controlled by chemicals that amoebas make themselves.

Had enough of microbes yet? Well, tough – they haven't had enough of you! At this very second there are several million crawling over your face and exploring your nostrils. And if you wanna know what else they're up to you'd better read on!

Because from now on it's gonna get personal…

MEDICAL MICROSCOPES

Where would modern medical science be without the microscope? Up a blind alley, that's where! Without microscopes scientists couldn't spot the more interesting little details of the body that really make it tick – like flakes of skin, for example. Chances are you've already seen a few of these disgusting details…

Imagine a summer's morning. A speck of dust dances in the sunlight like a gilded gnat. It's a perfect moment … *until you realize what dust is actually made of…*

DARE YOU DISCOVER ... WHAT DUST IS MADE OF?

You will need:

• a shaft of sunlight. (Draw some dark curtains allowing only a gap of 15 cm.) Alternatively, wait until night and use a small bright torch.

What you do:

1 Face the light.

2 Brush your hands through your hair, brush your hands over your arms, then lift your shirt and give it a shake.

What do you notice?

a) A cloud of black dots comes off me.

b) A cloud of shiny dots comes off me.

c) Huge chunks of skin fall off my body.

ANSWER

b) The dust specks are clumps of dead rotting flesh crawling with germs. Oh yes, they are. And they're all around you because you made them – they're your skin! If you saw **c)** consider the possibility that you're a vampire – in which case, sunlight could turn your body to dust!

BET YOU NEVER KNEW!

Specks of dust are some of the smallest things you can see. They're just 20 micrometres across and not much larger than bacteria. They're floating around all the time but you can't see them unless the light glints on them.

So, how well do you know your body? Just take a really close look at your hair, your eyes, your skin colour, the shape of your nose, the location of any moles or freckles. Spotted anything new? Well, in actual fact there's a lot you've never seen … the tiny bits.

COULD YOU BE A SCIENTIST?

Scientists estimate that you lose 50,000 bits of skin every minute. But the most incredible thing is that they've found that skin flakes from a man have about five times as many germs as skin flakes from a woman. Why? Is it because...

a) Male sweat has more food in it so more germs can live on male skin?
b) Men are dirtier than women?
c) Germs are killed by perfume on a woman's skin?

ANSWER

b) On average men take fewer baths than women. As you'll find out on page 180, washing gets rid of bacteria so women have fewer germs on their skin than men. And no, girls, that doesn't mean that boys are always smelly — they'd have to be really dirty and unwashed all the time with a lot more bacteria to be smelly. Award yourself half a mark if you said c) because perfume can kill germs in the areas where its applied to the skin.

Would you like to explore the human body in grisly detail? Well, if you're a bacterium you'd be doing this all the time and loving it! For bacteria, every day's a holiday…

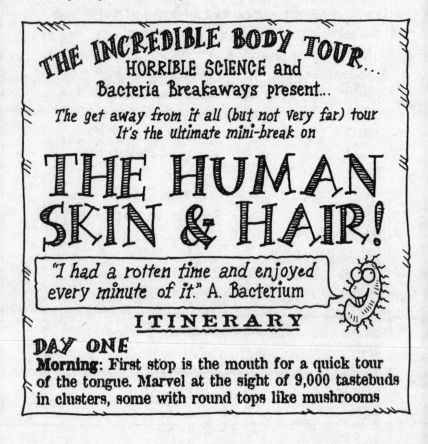

THE INCREDIBLE BODY TOUR…
HORRIBLE SCIENCE and
Bacteria Breakaways present…

The get away from it all (but not very far) tour
It's the ultimate mini-break on

THE HUMAN SKIN & HAIR!

"I had a rotten time and enjoyed every minute of it." A. Bacterium

ITINERARY

DAY ONE
Morning: First stop is the mouth for a quick tour of the tongue. Marvel at the sight of 9,000 tastebuds in clusters, some with round tops like mushrooms

and others pointed and ideal for moving food around. Enjoy the sight of the playful local bacteria frolicking amongst the tastebuds!

Afternoon: Sign up for the fascinating microbe safari. Watch the different bacteria in between the teeth. But beware – amoebas lurk in this area and they might try to eat you!

NOTES

1 Chinese leader Mao Tse-tung (1893–1976) never brushed his teeth and they eventually turned green. Eek by gum, I bet Mao just had to green and bear it.

2 The amoebas eat bacteria and are harmless to humans. One place to get a free amoeba is a dog's mouth. When a friendly dog gives you a big slobbery kiss you get an amoeba thrown in too.

DAY TWO

Morning: Enjoy a relaxing walking tour of the skin! Carefully does it – in some teenagers the skin pumps out half a bucket of oil a day so the going might get a bit slippery! Feel free to snack on the delicious oil and any dead bits of skin you might find.

Afternoon: Admire the volcanoes on the face plain. Well, they're not really volcanoes, they're pimples – so watch out when they erupt pus!

127

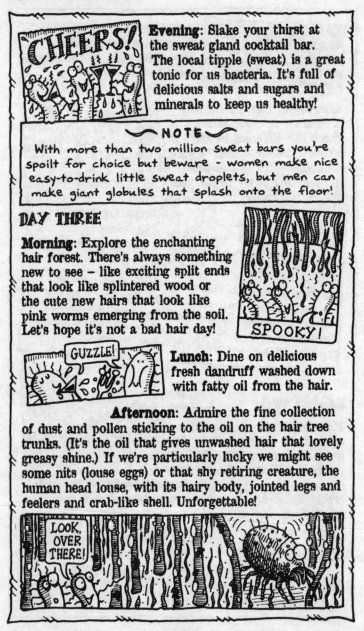

Evening: Slake your thirst at the sweat gland cocktail bar. The local tipple (sweat) is a great tonic for us bacteria. It's full of delicious salts and sugars and minerals to keep us healthy!

∽ NOTE ∽

With more than two million sweat bars you're spoilt for choice but beware - women make nice easy-to-drink little sweat droplets, but men can make giant globules that splash onto the floor!

DAY THREE

Morning: Explore the enchanting hair forest. There's always something new to see — like exciting split ends that look like splintered wood or the cute new hairs that look like pink worms emerging from the soil. Let's hope it's not a bad hair day!

SPOOKY!

GUZZLE!

Lunch: Dine on delicious fresh dandruff washed down with fatty oil from the hair.

Afternoon: Admire the fine collection of dust and pollen sticking to the oil on the hair tree trunks. (It's the oil that gives unwashed hair that lovely greasy shine.) If we're particularly lucky we might see some nits (louse eggs) or that shy retiring creature, the human head louse, with its hairy body, jointed legs and feelers and crab-like shell. Unforgettable!

LOOK, OVER THERE!

Evening: That's the end of the tour. Time to hop off the skin and take an air tour of the house before landing on the cat.

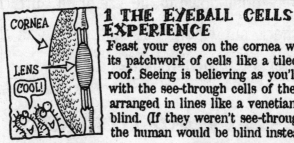

More tours

1 THE EYEBALL CELLS EXPERIENCE

Feast your eyes on the cornea with its patchwork of cells like a tiled roof. Seeing is believing as you'll see with the see-through cells of the lens arranged in lines like a venetian blind. (If they weren't see-through the human would be blind instead!)

2 THE BONE BREAKAWAY

Tour the eerie world inside the bones. The spongy bone inside the hard outer layer is like an immense cave system full of inter-connecting tunnels. You'd be a bone-head to miss it!

3 THE LONG LUNG WEEKEND

Visit the lungs for a breath of fresh air! Explore the tiny tubes into which air flows and admire the alveoli. These are the bags 0.01 cm across surrounded with blood vessels where oxygen goes into the blood and carbon dioxide flows out! Bags of fun for all the family!

WARNING: The walls of the tubes are lined with snot and you risk being stuck and then coughed up!

But if you didn't fancy taking a bacterial break then there's another way to see the human body. You could shrink down to the size of MI Gutzache. Let's check out where he's got to... Can you remember where we left him?

IT'S A SMALL WORLD! (CONTINUED)

The story so far. A shrinking experiment has gone horribly wrong and intrepid private eye Gutzache is floating in a cloud of snot...

Gutzache could see where he was going and he didn't relish it one bit. Tiny movements in the air puffed him towards the massive furry form of the Professor's cat, Tiddles. Gutzache drifted through a forest of tree trunks – at least, that's how it appeared to him. In fact, it was the fur on the cat's back.

Cats. Don't ask why but they're not my favourite animals. If things had worked out different I'd have taken my chances with organized crime. But I was on the cat and at least it was warm. Then she started licking herself. I felt rough but her tongue looked rougher - in fact, it was more like a giant rubbery sheet covered in cat dribble with spikes as long as my fingers.

So Gutzache was on Tiddles? How clever of her to rescue him! The cat's rough tongue acts like a comb separating the hairs and making glands in her skin produce oils that keep the fur in good condition. The spit dries (or evaporates as we scientists say) off the hairs, taking away heat and cooling her down.

Huh - the cat was cooling down but the heat was on me. That giant tongue got closer and closer. I smelt the hot fishy breath and I knew I was in for a licking...

LICK!

But just when all seemed lost Gutzache was rescued by a rather unlikely helper. Well, it wasn't so much of a helper as something that just came along and Gutzache grabbed hold of it and held on tight. It had a huge shield-shaped body about three times larger than Gutzache, covered in armoured plates. It had a dagger-like feeding tube and inside its see-through body Gutzache glimpsed a mass of freshly swallowed blood. Suddenly, the creature sprang high into the air – to Gutzache it seemed higher than a skyscraper. He had hitched a ride on a flea!

My whole life flashed before my eyes – it didn't make for pretty viewing. Then my stomach lurched as the flea touched down on another part of the cat's back. "Life's full of ups and downs," I thought, hastily jumping free and fleeing the flea.

I had no idea where Gutzache was and I was looking everywhere! I had divided the room into squares and I was searching each one using the strongest magnifying glass I could find. Where had he got to?

Nearer than you thought, Prof. Remember you were down on the floor and the cat came up? Maybe you remember stroking her and saying the words: "Naughty Tiddles, don't walk here - you might tread on Gutzache!" You didn't look too hard at your fingers afterwards - did you?

ER, NO!

Well, I was on one of them! You picked me up from the cat's back. You stood up - I was hollering like crazy, something like, "Listen up you stupid scientist I'm on your finger!" But you didn't hear me!

The Professor's skin was full of cracks like dried mud. Here and there tiny pits bubbled oily beads of moisture. Meanwhile Gutzache was sweating, too.

It was an ugly situation and the Prof wasn't too pretty neither. The hand was going up. I clung to a hair on the back of a finger. I knew it was going to be bad - I just didn't know how bad. But then I saw where we were headed and I knew. The giant mouth opened and a blast of hot air hit me. My stomach heaved - it smelt of sour milk, strong cheese, onions, garlic and old cow pats. Round globs of spit and slimy bacteria flew towards me. The Prof could sure use some mouthwash.

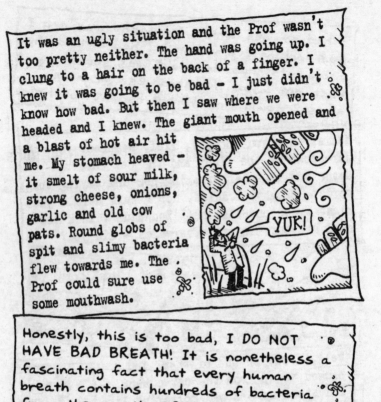

Honestly, this is too bad, I DO NOT HAVE BAD BREATH! It is nonetheless a fascinating fact that every human breath contains hundreds of bacteria from the mouth. Of course, I still had no idea that Gutzache was on my finger...

The Prof's nails didn't look in too good a shape. They were rough as tree bark and the ends were jagged. Bite marks I thought. I was right.

Helpless with horror, Gutzache watched as the Professor's finger was inserted into his giant mouth. The teeth looked like huge yellow cliffs and here and there slimy bacteria nestled in their folds and ridges. The teeth began to work backwards and forwards and the nail buckled and bent under the chewing action.

The job had become a gross-out. At that moment I longed to be anywhere but where I was. Well, maybe not anywhere – I'd give the Prof's guts a miss. Meantime, the Prof was making a meal of them fingernails. °❀⊛..

Actually, nails are made of keratin. Seen through an electron microscope keratin looks like a rope with smaller chemicals wound around it. This makes it very hard to tear and that's why my nail was buckling and not breaking.

Meanwhile Gutzache was right under the Professor's nose – literally. The finger didn't seem too safe so he decided to climb up a thick rope.

It turned out to be one of the Professor's nostril hairs and it was encrusted with dried snot. Feeling faint Gutzache swung himself into the hot, windy nostril and then clambered higher up the cheek.

The Prof and me were face to face but he still couldn't see me. He had some cheek! But the worst of all, his skin was crawling. It was oozing with slimy balls of bacteria that hid in tiny cracks. I figured I'd crack too if I stuck around. So I thought about it plenty but I couldn't figure how to escape...

OOOZE!

I had no idea all this time that Gutzache was on my face. Interestingly, over two million bacteria live on the cheeks and nose - and 72 million live in the grease on the forehead. Well, not that I've counted them ... but perhaps Gutzache could be persuaded to make a small survey...

Hey, I'd rather bungee jump off Brooklyn Bridge! The Prof still hadn't spotted me but something else had. It had a body like an armoured car and eight legs and a face that would sink a battleship. It wasn't too fast but for a minute I thought I was chicken-feed. But the bug wasn't too bothered – it was eating the squirming things off the Prof's skin. I said, "You're welcome pal!"

This is incredible! Gutzache is describing a demodex mite. These creatures, no more than 50 micrometres long, mostly live on human eyelashes and eyebrows. They do no harm and spread between people sharing towels so that every family has its very own special demodex family.

But things were about to get even worse for Gutzache. The Professor frowned as he wondered what to do next. He decided to resume his search of the floor, but the damage had been done. His skin rumpled and crinkled as if moved by an earthquake, and tiny chunks dislodged themselves and slipped into the air – a perfectly normal event caused by frowning. Once more, Gutzache felt himself falling helplessly – this time gripping on for dear life to what looked like a giant cornflake but was actually a flake of skin…

I was flying again and this time I figured I'd be ketchup. The room was spinning but my luck was in…

Gutzache landed on the very microscope slide that he had been sneezed off at the start of his adventure. And a minute or two later a familiar face peered down at him through the microscope…

I had found an interesting cat flea egg on the floor and I decided to take a closer look. Imagine my surprise to find Gutzache waiting for me. But he didn't look too happy...

IT'S A LONG STORY...

WHERE HAVE YOU BEEN?

The Prof enlarged me. He was talking about me taking a dip in a drop of pond water. Two seconds later I gave him my considered reply — "I don't swim," I snapped. And with that I quit. After what happened today it was small wonder ... a very, very small wonder.

FORGET IT!

If YOU don't fancy shrinking as small as Gutzache in order to check out some body bits, you could always peer at them through a microscope. Surgeons use microscopes all the time for what's called microsurgery. This can involve re-attaching bits and pieces of the body that have been chopped off by accident.

Hey – d'you fancy a bash at microsurgery? This quiz will have you in stitches!

COULD YOU BE A MICROSURGEON?

Unfortunately, your teacher has cut off his little finger. It happened whilst he was showing your class how to use a microtome. Even more unfortunately you're the only person who can help — but you've got to answer these questions correctly...

1 You hastily prepare an operating theatre. Why do you need a video camera and monitor linked up to a microscope?

a) So you can make a souvenir video to show your friends.

b) So you can see what you're doing without having to peer through the microscope all the time.

c) So other doctors can watch your progress and give you advice.

2 How do you protect your teacher's finger from bacteria?
a) Cook the finger. It smells bad but kills the germs.
b) Put it in the fridge but DON'T feed it to the cat.
c) Waggle the finger until the bacteria drop off.

3 OK, you're ready for the op but how are you going to re-attach the finger?
a) Superglue.
b) Sew it back on using a tiny needle.

c) Put it in a special bandage to hold it in place and wait two weeks for the finger to grow back on to the hand.

4 How do you join up the smaller blood vessels?
a) They're too small to bother about.
b) Melt the ends and weld them together.
c) Use a tiny staplegun.

5 After the op your teacher's finger needs a blood supply or it will die and rot and drop off. Keeping your teacher warm and giving him fluids helps. How do you deal with blockages in the finger's small veins?
a) Suspend your teacher upside down with his finger pointing downwards.

b) Get a huge hungry slimy leech to suck the blood from the little finger so that more rushes in.
c) Rub the finger so that the blood rushes into it.

ANSWERS

All the answers are **b).**

1 Sometimes surgeons use special microscopes with several eyepieces so that they can all see what's going on without shoving each other out of the way and taking turns.

2 Cold slows bacteria down. The finger should be kept moist in a germ-free bag floating in iced-water.

3 The trick is to use a tiny needle the size of this dash – with thread 0.2 mm wide to sew together all the nerves and blood vessels and bits of flesh that have been cut. Got all that? Good, well get going then. And no, you can't practise first.

4 Electrical probes are used for this delicate job.

5 It's true – leeches are often used after microsurgery because their spit contains a substance that stops blood clotting and keeps it on the move.

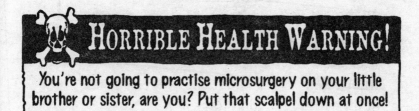

HORRIBLE HEALTH WARNING!

You're not going to practise microsurgery on your little brother or sister, are you? Put that scalpel down at once!

Even whilst the surgeons are battling to save your teacher's finger another group of scientists are glued to their microscopes as they take a closer look at the human body. Who are they and what are they up to? Well, I'd like to tell you now but I can't because ... the answer's in the next chapter!

SECRET CELLS

The amazing thing about the body is that the closer you look, the more you see. Seen close the body is an amazing landscape of hills and forests – oh all right, they're goosebumps and hairs – but seen closer still, it's an even more incredible assembly of … cells.

You remember cells? Robert Hooke was discovering them on page 81. Well, now it's time to look at animal and especially human cells. Here are the vital facts you need to get started…

Microscopic monsters fact file

Basic facts:
1 Plant cells have strong walls and food stores called vacuoles and animal cells don't. See what I mean...?

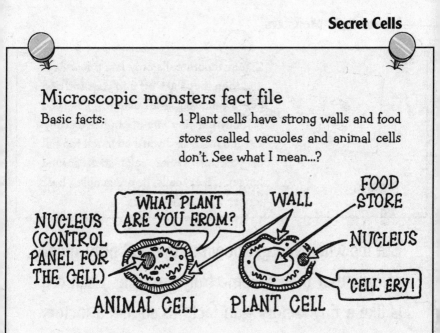

NUCLEUS (CONTROL PANEL FOR THE CELL)

WHAT PLANT ARE YOU FROM?

WALL

FOOD STORE

NUCLEUS

'CELL' ERY!

ANIMAL CELL

PLANT CELL

2 Your body is a collection of trillions of cells working together. And, as you're about to find out, some of them have special jobs to do.

Monstrous details
1 Every minute of the day millions of your cells die and millions more are made.

PHEW!

147

2 Your mouth cells only last a few days and then they flake off into your spit and get swallowed and eaten – so you actually eat tiny bits of your own body. Eat too many and you'd be much too full of yourself! Other cells stick around longer. Liver cells, for example, liver longer – up to five years.

But it's when you get down to the real nitty-gritty of cells that they become truly amazing. Each cell is like a tiny factory – in fact, it's so like a factory that you could imagine it is a factory. We've asked factory boss and Supreme Chief Executive Dick Taytor to guide us round...

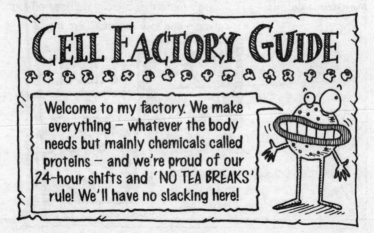

CELL FACTORY GUIDE

Welcome to my factory. We make everything – whatever the body needs but mainly chemicals called proteins – and we're proud of our 24-hour shifts and 'NO TEA BREAKS' rule! We'll have no slacking here!

FACTORY MAP...
MITOCHONDRIA
NUCLEUS
LYSOSOME
GOLGI COMPLEX
RIBOSOMES

SWEAT!

FACTORY WALL
WITH GATES
TO TAKE
SUPPLIES
IN AND
OUT.

ENDOPLASMIC
RETICULUM

STRAIN!

First stop, my office – known as
'THE NUCLEUS'. Here are the DNA
computers that send the orders to
those lazy workers on the shopfloor.

DO THIS!

DO THAT!

MITOCHONDRIA POWER STATIONS

GENERATE!

Here in the cell factory we generate our own
power. Don't ask me how we do it – I'm only
the boss! It's all done with glucose and oxygen
and the end-product is ATP* (That's a little
energy brick chemical that can be broken to
release power whenever it's
needed in the cell.)

KEEP OUT!

GOLGI COMPLEX
That's our storeroom
for proteins.

RIBOSOMES

TOIL!

This is where the real work
is done. The workers put
together protein that the
cell needs to grow. Nice
work guys and no, you
can't have a pay rise!

WORK!

***SCIENTIFIC NOTE...**
ATP is adenosine
triphosphate
(ad-deeno-sin
tri-foss-fate).
Say this in a
science lesson
and the shock
could make
your teacher's
wig fall off!

ENDOPLASMIC RETICULUM

(En-do-plas-mic ret-tick-u-lum) We're proud of this underground railway. It boosts productivity by taking proteins around the factory with maximum efficiency and minimal loss of productive capacity.

CHOO CHOO!

LYSOSOME WASTE PLANT

This is where we get rid of clapped out bits of the factory and I'm afraid we sometimes have to get rid of workers here too. But don't worry, they're dissolved in acid and it's quite painless really.

YOU'RE RUBBISH

CHEERS!

BUSINESS STRATEGY

When the factory gets too big we divide it down the middle into two separate enterprises. It's a big job because we have to copy everything in the factory including the nucleus and DNA computers but it's worth it to double production output.

STAGES OF DIVISION → CELL · CELL IN FIGURE OF 8 · TWO CELLS

BET YOU NEVER KNEW!

If a nucleus from a cell on the end of your nose was the size of your local park, the atoms that make up water will still be smaller than a postage stamp but your head would be the size of planet Earth! Know anyone that big-headed?

So you don't fancy working in the cell factory? Well, if you're looking for something to do, Dick Taytor has recommended some interesting openings for body cells…

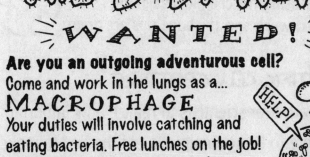

THE BODY NEWS

WANTED!

Are you an outgoing adventurous cell?
Come and work in the lungs as a…
MACROPHAGE
Your duties will involve catching and eating bacteria. Free lunches on the job! And you get to travel … up to the nose on the awesome giant-snot travelator!

HELP!

Are you a lazy slob? Do you enjoy hanging around? Then be a *FAT CELL!* Hold a globule of oily fat until the body needs it for energy. That's it. And you have a choice of living quarters – the sloppy stomach or the bulging bum! Plus all the free food you can eat!

WOBBLE!

Are you bone idle?
Well DON'T apply for this job!
We're after hard-working
OSTEOBLAST cells to build
up bones using the chemical calcium.
It's skilled work and the bone tips are great!

IT'S
A
BLAST!

SCIENTIFIC CELL-SPOTTERS

It took ages for scientists to realize how important cells were to living things. One of the first to make the connection was German scientist Theodor Schwann (1810–1882). Young Theo was a revoltingly good little child who was brilliant at school and kind to everyone he knew. YUCK! When he grew up he became a scientist and discovered that yeasts make alcoholic drinks by feeding on sugars and making alcohol. He also studied lots of bits of animals and found out that they were all made of cells. Unfortunately Schwann's views on yeasts were attacked by jealous rival scientists and he got so upset he gave up much of his work.

Gradually, with improved stains and microscopes scientists discovered many different types of cells in the body. But they lost their nerve with one type of cell ... the nerve cells. Nerves are your body's telephone wires that take messages to and from the brain – but they were hard to make sense of under the microscope.

That was before...

Hall of fame: Santiago Ramón y Cajal (1852–1934)
Nationality: Spanish

Young Santiago was a sensitive artistic lad who wanted to be an artist. His dad was less sensitive and less artistic and wanted his son to be a doctor, like him. But the boy rebelled and played truant from school. Don't try this – you might not get away with it.

Santiago didn't. He was punished by being sent to work for a shoemaker. (It must have given him a terrible sense of de-feet.) Santiago decided that medicine wasn't so bad after all, and so the boy and his dad studied medicine together. But they had a problem – to study bones they needed human skeletons. They were too poor to buy bones so what did they do?

a) Made shoes and sold them to buy bones.

b) Killed people and studied their bones.

c) Dug up bones in the local churchyard.

ANSWER

c) This was a grave crime and they had to do it at the *dead* of night – geddit? If the local priest had found out he'd have had a bone to pick with the pair of them!

After boning up on his medical knowledge Santiago's dad became a professor and after a spell in the army medical service Santiago studied at his dad's university. By the 1880s Santiago was really into microscopes, but he had a problem. Here's what his diary might have looked like…

156

JANUARY 1888

These nerves are getting on my nerves. I'm trying to study them but they're all tangled up and I can't see where one begins and one ends. Scientists reckon they're long fibres like bits of string but its hard to be sure and I'm getting in a real tangle! I'm a bag of nerves!

FEBRUARY 1888

I've heard about a new discovery by Italian scientist, Camillo Golgi.* He was mixing up chemicals in a hospital kitchen and cooked up this stain to show nerves clearly. It's based on silver nitrate. Hmm, I thought, that was the chemical used to develop photos. It could be an exciting development, but all the other scientists think it's useless.

MARCH 1888

mumble!

mutter, moan!

WOW AND WOW AGAIN! It was tough to get the stain to work - it's hard to mix and get the right quantity. But I've done it - and guess what! I can see the nerves clearly! I was really nervous that it wouldn't work but now I can see that the nerves are a network of cells. I can't wait to tell everyone!

APRIL 1888

I don't believe it - I've sent my account of the discovery to a science magazine and they haven't

* Yes, he was something to do with the Golgi complex — he discovered it!

published it! What happens if someone makes the same discovery and grabs the glory first?

MAY 1888 — NERVOUS TREMBLE! →

I know what I'll do. I'll publish my own magazine! It'll be full of fascinating articles about me, EXCELLENT! saying how clever I am and everything, and I can also publish the account of my discovery! It's going to cost a lot but I'm sure my wife and children can go without food for a bit...

The magazine was in Spanish, a language most foreign scientists didn't understand, but eventually the news of the discovery got around. Santiago became famous, and in 1906 he and Golgi were awarded the Nobel Prize. But they were still arguing about nerves because Golgi still reckoned they were fibres.

Mind you, looking at dead nerve cells isn't half as scary as peering at the creatures in the next chapter. They're the most disgustingly ugly microscopic monsters of them all! Unfortunately these little monsters share your home and no, I'm NOT talking about your little brother or sister!

Will your nerve hold for the next chapter?

HIDDEN HORRORS IN YOUR HOME

This is a chapter about the microscopic monsters that haunt your home and skulk in your supper. So, is your home as safe as houses? Better read on and find out!

Well, one thing's certain: things are better than they used to be. Almost 400 years ago a guest was shocked at the condition of his host's house. The famous writer Erasmus looked down and saw:

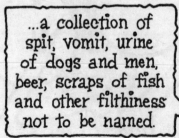

...a collection of spit, vomit, urine of dogs and men, beer, scraps of fish and other filthiness not to be named.

In those days every house was this dirty and every house must have been a microbe's paradise. (Hopefully your house is a bit cleaner.) But even today, no matter how clean a house appears, there are horrible microscopic surprises in store.

Like these.

FIVE HIDDEN HORRORS IN YOUR HOME

1 For every 0.03 cubic metres of air in your home there are 300,000 tiny floating lumps of grit, dead skin, ash and rubber. You breathe this lot in all the time but luckily most of it gets stuck in your wonderful snotty throat.

2 Have you got a cat? If so, when it licks itself tiny globules of spit will be released in invisible clouds. In a few hours of grooming your cat will have produced several billion balls of spit that float gracefully through the air and splatter every surface in the house with kitty drool.

3 If you've got a dog your house may be littered with dog hairs. You'll get more of them in the spring when the dog moults and you might see there are two different types: ordinary hairs and longer hairs that help protect the others and help them trap warm air next to the dog's skin. Oh, nearly forgot – attached to the hairs you'll find clumps of rotting doggie dandruff.

4 And that's not all. If you're really unlucky your dog might have dog lice. There'll be tiny eggs on the hairs and lots of little 1.5-mm-long flea-like creatures keen to explore your home and make new friends.

ALL DOGS ARE LOUSY!

5 Under your carpet you might find 'woolly bears'. No, these aren't large grizzly teddies that roam the forests of North America – they're grisly little carpet-beetle grubs that happily chomp their way through your carpets. They relish a nice dollop of cat fluff or dog hair or even human hair – well, carpets for breakfast, lunch and supper must get a bit boring. Mind you, if your parents find them they'll be chewing the carpet too.

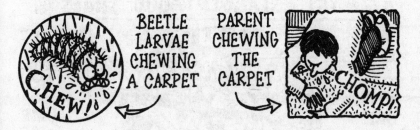

BEETLE LARVAE CHEWING A CARPET

PARENT CHEWING THE CARPET

But that's nothing. *Nothing* compared to what else lurks in your carpets…

DISGUSTING DUST

The grey dust in a vacuum cleaner bag looks gross. But to discover its scary secrets you'll need to peer through the microscope at this disgusting dust blob. Go on, you know you want to...

OH THAT IS SO YUCK!

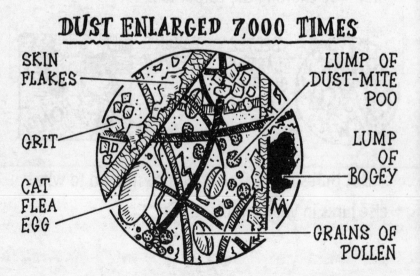

DUST ENLARGED 7,000 TIMES

SKIN FLAKES

GRIT

CAT FLEA EGG

LUMP OF DUST-MITE POO

LUMP OF BOGEY

GRAINS OF POLLEN

BET YOU NEVER KNEW!

Your home is swarming with tiny creatures called dust mites. These bugs don't do any harm but we can breathe in their poo and this can trigger asthma attacks in some people, which make breathing hard. And the really bad news is that dust mites poo 20 times a day (If they used toilet paper it would cost a fortune!)

COULD YOU BE A SCIENTIST?

In 1973 physician Dr Robert Haddock found a fishy mystery on the island of Guam. Cases of food poisoning by salmonella bacteria were soaring but why? The islanders were eating the same food as usual — it was mostly brought to the island in tins and free of bacteria. So how were bacteria getting into the food? Eventually the doctor discovered the truth.

But what was it?

a) People weren't washing their hands after visiting the toilet and the germs were on their hands when they cooked the food.

b) Cats were spreading the germs by leaping on to the dinner table and dribbling over the food.

c) Vacuum cleaners were sucking up the germs and spraying them everywhere.

ANSWER

c) Yes – I'm sorry to say that when you vacuum the floor tiny things like germs get sucked in the cleaner and because they're very small they get through the bag and the filter and out the exhaust pipe and spray all over you. Actually it's even *worse* than that because along with the germs emerges a huge cloud of mite poo from the mites in the carpet! Meantime any sucked-up baby mites stay in the cleaner bag and happily dine on the vast collection of scrumptious dead skin they find there!

☠ HORRIBLE HEALTH WARNING!

What are you saying, "yuck" for? You've helped with the hoovering haven't you? It didn't kill you – did it? Well, your body can fight off the germs and the mite poo mostly gets stuck in the snot of your nose and throat so it's not an excuse to refuse to help with the cleaning.

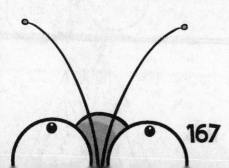

BET YOU NEVER KNEW!

Hold on to this book, sit down and take a deep breath. Ready now? I've got a bit of bad news ... you know those revolting mite things in the carpet? Well, they're not just in the carpet. There's some in your bed and in your pillow and there's even worse news to come ... you'd best read on!

A quick note to the reader...

Remember what I said about bacteria? Don't panic! Mites have been living with humans since the day when people lived in caves and the Internet was just a smart way to catch mammoths. And they've never done us any harm! (That's the mites not the mammoths.)

Let's imagine a dust mite wrote letters to her friend on the carpet. OK, I know this is a mite silly – after all I expect dust mites use mobile phones these days...

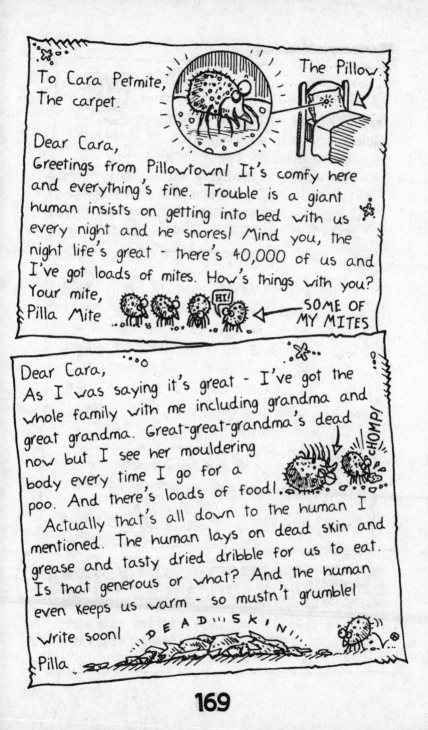

To Cara Petmite,
The carpet.

The Pillow.

Dear Cara,
Greetings from Pillowtown! It's comfy here
and everything's fine. Trouble is a giant
human insists on getting into bed with us
every night and he snores! Mind you, the
night life's great - there's 40,000 of us and
I've got loads of mites. How's things with you?
Your mite,
Pilla Mite

HI!

SOME OF
MY MITES

Dear Cara,
As I was saying it's great - I've got the
whole family with me including grandma and
great grandma. Great-great-grandma's dead
now but I see her mouldering
body every time I go for a
poo. And there's loads of food!

CHOMP!

Actually that's all down to the human I
mentioned. The human lays on dead skin and
grease and tasty dried dribble for us to eat.
Is that generous or what? And the human
even keeps us warm - so mustn't grumble!

Write soon!

Pilla

DEAD SKIN

169

Dear Cara,

A terrible day! And it started *DRIBBLE!* so well – the cat slept on the pillow and left delicious globs of dried spit for our breakfast! The interesting fishy flavour makes a change from all that dead skin! Anyway, I puffed out a bit of gas *PUFF!* from my bum (no it wasn't a fart, silly, it was a chemical signal to the family to come and eat) and I saw the huge jaws...

A cheyletus. I don't have to tell you what these bugs do to us dust mites! It was after me but I got away. It grabbed my little sister and gobbled her up! I always used to argue with my sister but she went down a treat with the monster. Well, if I can't be safe in my own bed where can I be safe? I've crawled into the human's clothes and when the human gets into them I'm off to seek my fortune. See you on the carpet.

Your mite,   Pilla   *BYE!*

☠ HORRIBLE HEALTH WARNING!

Pillow mites don't do any harm and if you make a fuss about going to bed you'll probably be given a block of wood for a pillow. Oh well, you'll sleep like a log!

Mind you, there are more mites in your home than you mite think. There's a *mitey* BIG number ... and there are lots of other bugs too!

THE HORRIBLE SCIENCE

ERR! YIKES! HELP! YUK! UGH!

NOT-VERY-IDEAL HOME EXHIBITION

BEDROOM
Up to 2,000,000 mites in a double bed.

BEDROOM
Red spider mite sneaks in from the garden to spend the winter indoors.

KITCHEN
Flour mites snack on your breakfast cereal

BEDROOM
Mangy cat fur caused by itch mite that burrows into Tiddles' flesh. (That's a cat-astrophe!)

LIVING ROOM
Booklice feed on old books.

KITCHEN
Bird mite refuses to budgie from your budgie

And that's not all… Not surprisingly, your house is *bulging* with bacteria. They're oozing over the furniture and slurping into the wallpaper and in the kitchen they're slobbering and squelching in your food. Dinner anyone?

THE MICROBE
GOOD FOOD GUIDE...
By Mike Robe

Hi micro-munchers! There's nothing that we bacteria like better than a little nibble of nosh but we all suffer little dinner-time disasters. I'll never forget the day I tried to eat disinfectant! Anyway, here's our guide to the smartest and cheapest places to eat out as sampled by our team of inspectors — the slime squad!

A word about safety...
Safety is very important. Every year billions of bacteria suffer fatal accidents which could have been prevented by a little safety awareness. Things to beware of when eating out...

1 BLEACH Run a mile – and if you can't manage a mile, you'd better squirm a few millimetres. BLEACH WILL KILL YOU INSTANTLY!

2 SALT Don't eat too much of this. You'll find that your body will suck in water to dilute the salt and you'll explode!

THE KITCHEN BIN BISTRO

The classic eatery! A must for all gourmet bacteria. Easily the most wide-ranging menu, plus old favourites such as 'cat food and cold mashed potato cottage pie' and 'dad's cooking's gone wrong again' and that all-time favourite 'last night's leftover curry'. For pudding why not try slimy yoghurt scum? Recommended!

A cheap and cheerful watering hole with a smelly atmosphere all of its own. Here you can relax in the moist surroundings and dine on a delightful range of dishes including mouldy breadcrumb surprise and greasy fat soup.

THE DISHCLOTH DINER

THE COLD STEW CAFÉ

Delicious boiled meat and vegetables proved easy to digest with just a sprinkling of salt (but thankfully not enough to spoil the taste). There were delicious and tempting extras on offer such as 'fresh fungi and mite-poo pudding'. No wonder the restaurant was packed with bacteria! Recommended!

THE TIN CAN HOTEL (guests only)

No bacteria are allowed past the strong metal walls! Conditions inside are said to be grim with no atmosphere at all! Actually we found out that bacteria do eat there but they're guests and sometimes they trash the place and cause nasty stinks.

~ SCIENTIFIC NOTE ~
These bacteria don't need oxygen to live.

The chemicals on the staff were a really hard-boiled lot and made us feel unwelcome – and that's no yolk – er, joke. One of our team was so badly treated that she dissolved! Best avoided.

THE GOLDEN EGG

~ SCIENTIFIC NOTE ~
Eggs contain chemicals that dissolve bacteria.

I'm afraid this was another eatery that didn't live up to its initial promise. Although there was delicious fat on the menu the service was rather cold and eventually we felt we were being frozen out.

Now you've had your meal, how about ruining your teacher's lunch?

☠ HORRIBLE HEALTH WARNING!

This may not be very wise. If you get expelled for doing this you don't know me, OK?

The HORRIBLE SCIENCE guide to PUTTING TEACHERS OFF THEIR LUNCH

Step one – Make sure you sit at the same table as your teacher. Bellowing these facts across the canteen could get you into even worse trouble.

Step two – During the meal it's important to make sure that your table manners are perfect.

Things not to do...**DO NOT** pick your nose. **DO NOT** eat with your mouth open or smack your lips. **DO NOT** burp and wipe your greasy mouth on your sleeve...good luck!

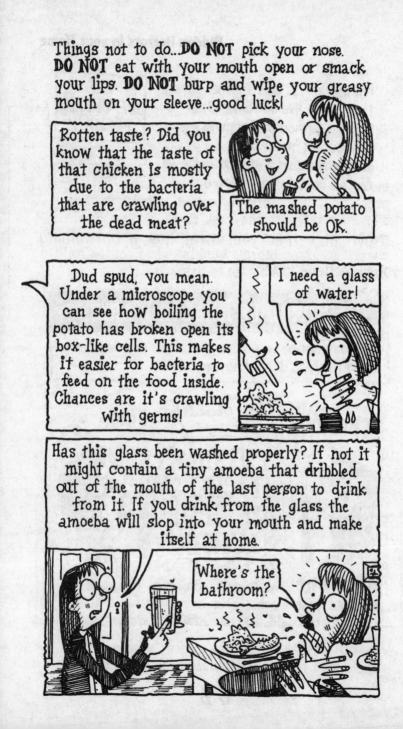

Rotten taste? Did you know that the taste of that chicken is mostly due to the bacteria that are crawling over the dead meat?

The mashed potato should be OK.

Dud spud, you mean. Under a microscope you can see how boiling the potato has broken open its box-like cells. This makes it easier for bacteria to feed on the food inside. Chances are it's crawling with germs!

I need a glass of water!

Has this glass been washed properly? If not it might contain a tiny amoeba that dribbled out of the mouth of the last person to drink from it. If you drink from the glass the amoeba will slop into your mouth and make itself at home.

Where's the bathroom?

BET YOU NEVER KNEW!

If you looked at milk under a powerful microscope it wouldn't be white! The white colour comes from blobs of a chemical called casein that contains proteins. The casein reflects the light to give a white colour. But the rest of the liquid is clear water with blobs of yellow fat and smaller chemicals and minerals bobbing about in the milk. Have YOU got the bottle to drink it?

TEACHER'S TEA-BREAK TEASER
Try this one and you'll be as welcome as a woodworm in a wooden leg factory … so don't forget to SMILE. Pound your fists on the staffroom door. When it opens your teacher will be desperately clutching a well-earned cup of tea. Ask them:

ANSWER

When you boil a kettle there are bound to be bacteria in the water. They may have got into the kettle from the air or they may have been in the water. As the water heats up the bacteria will start to feel warm and comfy. But the growing heat will burn their tiny hairs and melt their slimy bodies. This is a very cruel fate even for bacteria. How can your teacher stomach drinking tea flavoured with murdered melted germs?

Mind you, if this talk of slimy bacteria has you dashing to the toilet I've got bad news. The bacteria have got there first and you're about to encounter THE ULTIMATE HORROR!

Dare you face…

THE TERROR IN YOUR TOILET! ➤

TERROR IN THE TOILET

If bacteria are getting under your skin or on your skin or up your nose or anywhere else, what should you do?

a) Pick your nose and spots.

b) Get someone else to pick your nose and spots.

c) Wash the bacteria off.

ANSWER

c) Probably – or as a scientist would say ... "yes and no". Let's face a few facts before reaching for that bar of soap...

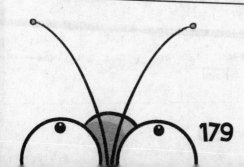

Microscopic monsters fact file

Name:

Basic facts:

Washing and germs

1 Most people think that soap kills germs, but in fact most people are wrong. Soap doesn't usually kill germs, but it does send them on a one-way trip to the sewer. Here's how...

2 Washing your hands in water won't get rid of germs because they cling to the greasy surface of the skin. The water and grease don't mix so nothing happens.

3 Tiny bits of soap (scientists call them molecules) consist of a 'head' containing sodium and a 'tail' made of chemicals called hydrocarbons (hi-dro-car-bons).

GERMS

GREASE

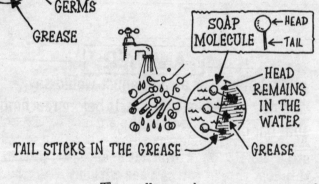

SOAP MOLECULE ← HEAD
← TAIL

HEAD REMAINS IN THE WATER

TAIL STICKS IN THE GREASE — GREASE

This allows the water to wash grease, soap and germs down the plug-hole!

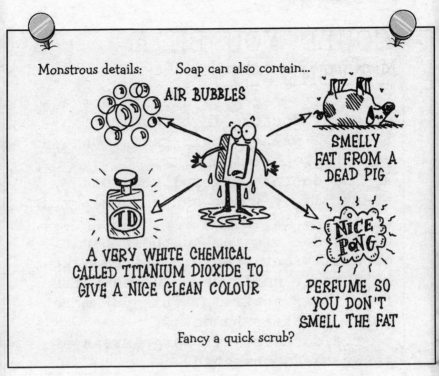

Monstrous details: Soap can also contain...

AIR BUBBLES

SMELLY FAT FROM A DEAD PIG

A VERY WHITE CHEMICAL CALLED TITANIUM DIOXIDE TO GIVE A NICE CLEAN COLOUR

NICE PONG

PERFUME SO YOU DON'T SMELL THE FAT

Fancy a quick scrub?

BET YOU NEVER KNEW!

The soap will make bubbles on your hands as layers of soap and water trap air. Oh, so you've noticed? Well, take a good look at the surface of the bubble. At just 50 micrometres thick – it's thinner than a stick insect on a diet. It's actually one of the thinnest things you can see without a microscope.

COULD YOU BE A SCIENTIST?

Scientists secretly studied how a group of doctors in an Australian hospital washed their hands. What do you think they found?

a) The doctors carefully washed every bit of their hands to get rid of any germs.

b) The doctors washed their hands carefully but then did things like bite their nails and plucked hairs from their nostrils. This put more germs on their hands.

c) The doctors left large areas of their hands unwashed.

ANSWER:

c) Doctors always missed these regions:

LOADS OF BACTERIA FROM NOSE ON THIS FINGER (HAND-PICKED!)

Next time you wash your hands think carefully about what you're doing. Did you miss any vital bits?

Not surprisingly, the bathroom is like a nature reserve for microbe wildlife. Fancy a tour?

Come to the HORRIBLE SCIENCE

MICRO-SAFARI PARK!

Lots of fun for all the family... in fact it's so much fun you won't be able to get them out of the bathroom even when you want to go to the toilet!

1 EXPLORE THE EXCITING BLACK MOULD FOREST!
The black spots you can see are actually the structures that make spores to make more black moulds whilst the little feeding tubes underneath eat your bathroom!

OOER!

❷ GO SCUBA DIVING in the romantic sink overflow – it's the place in the bathroom which has more germs than any other!

❸ CLIMB THE TOOTHBRUSH! It's crawling with germs – if you're lucky you'll spot a mouth-amoeba eating the bacteria!

CHOMP!

❹ EXPLORE THE TOWELS for stray dust mites and demodex creatures.

MUNCH!

❺ THE DOOR KNOB is a wonderful place to spot germs especially after someone's had a poo and not washed their hands properly. (One in five toilet door knobs have tiny lumps of poo on.)

PHWOAR!

CHEW!

❻ FEEDING TIME AT THE SOAP BAR. If it's wet you should see lots of germs happily eating the soap!

7 Round off your visit with a trip to the taps to be entertained by the amazing *TAP-DANCING BACTERIA!*

TAP! TAP! TAP! TAP!

8 Grand Finale: Marvel at the *TOILET FLUSH-FOUNTAIN* as it showers you with tiny droplets of water and pee and germs and lumps of poo...

PLOP!

FLUSH!

Smellie School
Greater Whiffing
Dear Sir,
I would like to complain about your book where it says that toilets spray germs and other unmentionable matter. As a result of your book no one's dared to flush the toilets in our school for six weeks and the situation is getting desperate. Excuse me as I adjust my clothes-peg on my nose. This time you've really gone too far! It's not even true ... is it?
Yours crossly,
Mrs Head (Head)

Well Mrs Head, I'M AFRAID IT'S TRUE...
Admittedly the droplets are too small to see – a
few micrometres across. But just for you, Mrs Head,
here's an experiment designed to make them
visible. We've recruited fearless private eye MI
Gutzache to flush this toilet.

The water has been stained with a brown dye and
when you turn the lights off the dye glows in the
dark. Mind you, the toilet hasn't been cleaned for a
few months so we hope that brown stuff in the

water is just the dye. We've also rigged up a high-speed camera with special high-speed film capable of photographing microscopic droplets flying about in the dark…

Oh well, now for the moment of truth!

THE DEADLY EXPLODING TOILET EXPERIMENT

Here's Gutzache just about to flush the toilet…

THIS AIN'T NO BIG DEAL!

DANGER! DO NOT FLUSH!

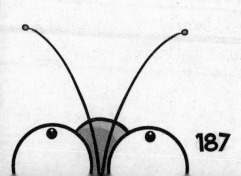

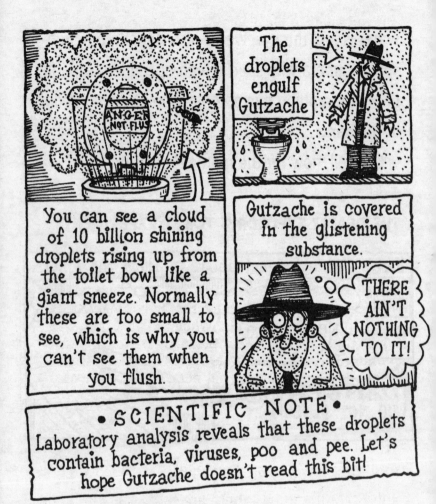

You can see a cloud of 10 billion shining droplets rising up from the toilet bowl like a giant sneeze. Normally these are too small to see, which is why you can't see them when you flush.

The droplets engulf Gutzache

Gutzache is covered in the glistening substance.

THERE AIN'T NOTHING TO IT!

• SCIENTIFIC NOTE •
Laboratory analysis reveals that these droplets contain bacteria, viruses, poo and pee. Let's hope Gutzache doesn't read this bit!

A quick note to the reader...

Scared yet?

1 DON'T try flushing the chain with the lid down. Apparently this makes the cloud of droplets and germs worse because it squirts out under the lid with greater force.

2 DO flush the loo yourself – no, don't bribe your little brother/ sister to do it or leave you-know-whats bobbing about in the loo. And don't be scared! Your body fights off the germs.

BET YOU NEVER KNEW!

You'll remember from page 11 that paper consists of tiny fibres? Well, the loosely woven fibres of toilet paper leave lots of holes. The holes soak up water and since poo is 75 per cent water, germs can easily hide in microscopic droplets that soak on to your hands. When toilet paper was invented in 1857 it was made out of tough paper which didn't let water through. Trouble is, it was very harsh on the poor old bum, whilst the looser fibres of modern toilet paper feel softer.

And whilst we're on the toilet – I mean on the *subject* of the toilet – here are some facts that you definitely shouldn't read aloud at mealtimes...

EIGHT MICROSCOPIC FACTS THAT YOU ALWAYS WANTED TO KNOW ABOUT TOILETS AND NEVER DARED ASK...

• Public toilet urinals (the things that men pee in) often spray back microscopic drops of pee on to shoes and trousers. This can be a wee bit embarrassing.

• The nasty sharp smell in dirty public toilets is probably ammonia. This is a chemical produced by bacteria which they make by eating another chemical found in pee called urea. You might be interested to know that ammonia is great for growing plants but when babies get it on their skin it causes nappy rash.

• In Roman times the ammonia from pee was used to make mouthwash and toothpaste. Fancy a gargle?

CHOKE!

WE RAN OUT OF PEE SO I MADE THIS BATCH FROM POO

• In some places in the USA toilet seats are covered in disposable paper to protect your bum from germs. Actually there aren't that many germs on toilet seats. Maybe they get squashed when people with large bottoms sit on them.

• Are you keen on saving paper? One of the cleanest toilets in the world is a Japanese invention that sprays your bum with water and dries it with hot air so you don't need any toilet paper. It even sprays scent on your bum to give it a nice fresh smell.

• Alternatively, if you really want to look after the environment why not buy a compost loo? There's lots of versions available. On one Dutch invention you can rock back and forward whilst you sit on the toilet. (You might as well take a radio in and listen to rock and roll music while you're at it.) The rocking motion mixes the poo with soil inside the toilet. Within a few weeks germs rot the poo into lovely fertilizer for the garden!

• Much of the nasty smell in farts is from chemicals made by germs that live in the gut. Oh, so you knew that? Well, did you know that farting *killed* one man? Eighteenth-century star Simon 'Bellows' Tup was known as 'the farting blacksmith'. He sang songs to the sound of his amazing musical farts. His bottom could even squeal like the bagpipes. Sadly, one night Simon's version of "Blow high and blow low" proved too much. He burst a blood vessel and died for his fart ... er, I mean art.

• One night in 1856, Matthew Gladman went to the toilet in his home town of Lewes, England. Unfortunately the floor of the toilet had been removed prior to cleaning the pit underneath. Down Matthew fell into a deep pit of doo-doo... Gladman wasn't a glad man! He died of suffocation by methane gas from the germs as they fed on the rotting poo.

Of course, things have improved since those days. Nowadays your school toilets are not placed above a deep pit full of poo (and children are no longer thrown in when they're naughty). Chances are they're connected up to a sewage works. And when it comes to getting rid of big jobs the tiny microbes have a BIG JOB!

BET YOU NEVER KNEW!
At sewage works sewage is rotted down by a range of bacteria that eat the poo and paper. OK, so you knew that? Well, did you know that scientists have found that bacteria in sewage are very good at making vitamin B12, a chemical that helps build healthy nerve cells. In fact, if you take a vitamin supplement the B12 may have been made by these bacteria!

Actually, this is just one of many discoveries made as scientists learn more about the microscopic world. But what are these discoveries and where are they taking us? Is small really going to be beautiful or are we heading for a GINORMOUS monster disaster?

Time to leave this chapter and start the next page…

WASH YOUR HANDS FIRST!

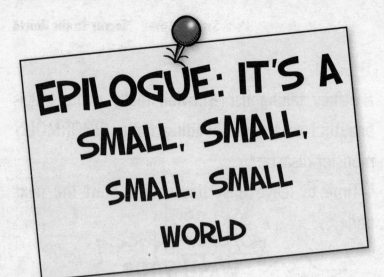

EPILOGUE: IT'S A SMALL, SMALL, SMALL, SMALL WORLD

Some people think BIG. Big plans, big ideas, big money and they often have big heads to match. Other people think small and amongst them are many scientists who believe that microscopic technology holds the tiny little key to our future... But will these plans work out...?

Well, the only way to be sure is to go and see and that means time travel into the future. As luck would have it, Professor N Large has been working on a time machine and the obvious person to test it is fearless investigator MI Gutzache...

Oh all right, maybe we'll have to experiment on an animal. Perhaps Tiddles can be coaxed into trying it...

I am keen to discover the future direction of micro-research. I've written a letter to future scientists to introduce Tiddles and fitted her with a video camera to record her experiences in the year 2050.

Dear Future Colleague,

This is to introduce my cat, Tiddles, who I have sent into the future to test my time-machine and return with a record of micro-technology in your time. Please help her with the video controls and send her back in one piece.

Thanks a lot,

Prof N Large

ARE YOU READY TIDDLES?

POP!

Dear Prof N Large

Thanks for your letter. We couldn't work out how to work that funny old-fashioned video camera. Anyway, we sorted it out in the end.

Prof I B Smalle

And here's the video Tiddles brought back...

Hi Prof. Things are great in 2050! Thanks to micro-technology, we've solved the world food problem! Everyone now eats chlorella algae — you can grow it much faster than any other food. It tastes like spinach but hey — you get used to it!

Anyway, you can genetically engineer it to look and taste like anything — even cat food!

SCIENTIFIC NOTE...
Genetic engineering involves adding new bits to the DNA of bacteria. The new DNA programs the microbes to make any protein chemical you like. One example is human growth-hormone. (Oddly enough, that's the substance that makes people grow.) In the past, people who couldn't make enough were treated with injections of the stuff taken from dead bodies. Now back to the future...

And now, thanks to genetic engineering, we grow elastin — as you know that's the stretchy substance in your body found around joints and elsewhere. Anyway, its great for making bandages and new blood vessels!

And right now genetically engineered bacteria are being produced for space travel! They eat astronauts' poo and pee and turn it into delicious snack bars which they can eat again! Yum yum!

And micro-technology is BIG BUSINESS NOW. My favourite game is nanofootball. You use a nanomanipulator — a super-powerful virtual reality electron-microscope with 3D graphics that makes you feel you're kicking atoms about! It's cool!

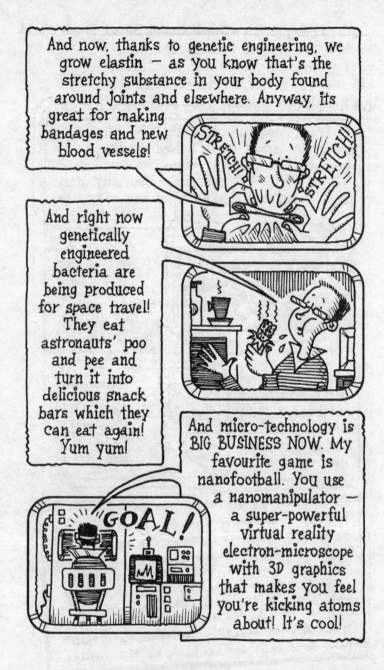

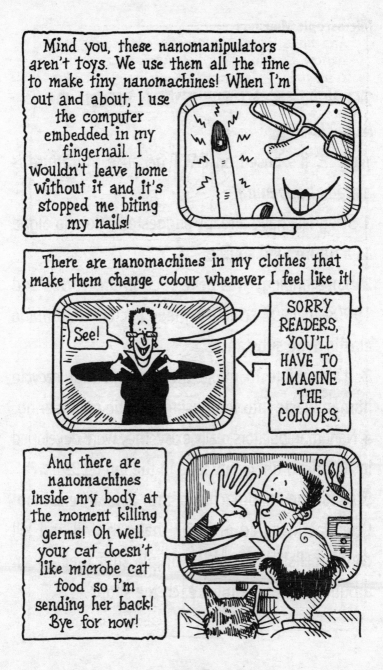

Mind you, these nanomanipulators aren't toys. We use them all the time to make tiny nanomachines! When I'm out and about, I use the computer embedded in my fingernail. I wouldn't leave home without it and it's stopped me biting my nails!

There are nanomachines in my clothes that make them change colour whenever I feel like it!

See!

SORRY READERS, YOU'LL HAVE TO IMAGINE THE COLOURS.

And there are nanomachines inside my body at the moment killing germs! Oh well, your cat doesn't like microbe cat food so I'm sending her back! Bye for now!

199

SO YOU DON'T BELIEVE A WORD OF ALL THIS?

Well ... it's based on FACT *because the future is already happening*!

1 Scientists have already suggested chlorella algae as a future food source.

2 Biotechnology was developed in the 1980s and 1990s. In 1996 scientists made bacteria that made elastin-type substances.

3 It's possible to make the bacteria that recycle human waste into food using genetic engineering.

4 Nanomanipulators really exist! They were developed in American university labs in the later 1990s.

5 As for the nanomachines, they actually exist too! One was invented in 2017 that can drill and kill cancer cells! Here's some simple stuff that's been around long enough to reach the shops...

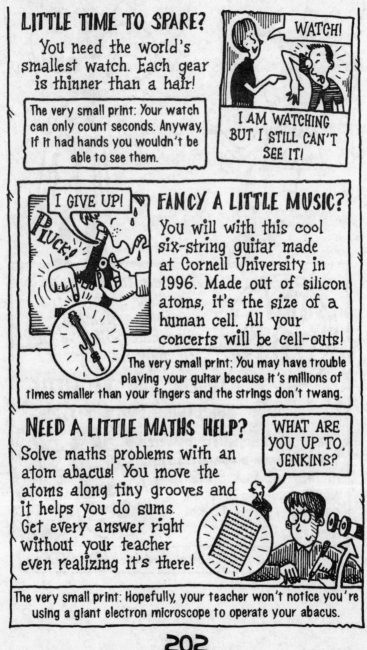

LITTLE TIME TO SPARE?

You need the world's smallest watch. Each gear is thinner than a hair!

The very small print: Your watch can only count seconds. Anyway, if it had hands you wouldn't be able to see them.

WATCH!

I AM WATCHING BUT I STILL CAN'T SEE IT!

I GIVE UP!

PLUCK!

FANCY A LITTLE MUSIC?

You will with this cool six-string guitar made at Cornell University in 1996. Made out of silicon atoms, it's the size of a human cell. All your concerts will be cell-outs!

The very small print: You may have trouble playing your guitar because it's millions of times smaller than your fingers and the strings don't twang.

NEED A LITTLE MATHS HELP?

Solve maths problems with an atom abacus! You move the atoms along tiny grooves and it helps you do sums. Get every answer right without your teacher even realizing it's there!

WHAT ARE YOU UP TO, JENKINS?

The very small print: Hopefully, your teacher won't notice you're using a giant electron microscope to operate your abacus.

These tiny inventions could do with a tiny bit of improvement. But they've got BIG potential. So what about the future? Is tomorrow full of BIG POSSIBILITIES? Or are the scientists just being small-minded?

Well, who can say? One thing's for certain - right now microscopes are helping scientists to explore the world of microscopic monsters like never before. In fact, thanks to microscopes, we can all see these monsters' horribly tiny world. And once you've peered down the eyepiece of a microscope and seen this strange place, the ordinary everyday world will never be the same again...

Well, what can I say, that's Horrible Science for you!

HORRIBLE INDEX